Dressed in Knits

— · 19 · —

Designs for Creating a Custom Knitwear Collection

ALEX CAPSHAW-TAYLOR

 INTERWEAVE.
interweave.com

fw
a content + ecommerce company

www.fwcommunity.com

10 9 8 7 6 5 4 3 2 1

Distributed in Canada by Fraser Direct
100 Armstrong Avenue
Georgetown, ON, Canada L7G 5S4
Tel: (905) 877-4411

Distributed in the U.K. and Europe by
F&W MEDIA INTERNATIONAL
Brunel House, Newton Abbot, Devon,
TQ12 4PU, England
Tel: (+44) 1626 323200,
Fax: (+44) 1626 323319
E-mail: enquiries@fwmedia.com

Distributed in Australia by
Capricorn Link
P.O. Box 704, S. Windsor NSW, 2756
Australia
Tel: (02) 4560 1600, Fax: (02) 4577 5288
E-mail: books@capricornlink.com.au

SRN: 15KN10
ISBN-13: 978-1-62033-946-6

PDF SRN: EP9448
PDF ISBN-13: 978-1-62033-947-3

EDITOR
Ann Budd

TECHNICAL EDITOR
Lori Gayle

ASSISTANT ART DIRECTOR
Charlene Tiedemann

COVER & INTERIOR DESIGN
Bekah Thrasher

PHOTOGRAPHER
Joe Hancock

PHOTO STYLIST
Allie Liebgott

HAIR & MAKEUP
Kathy MacKay

PRODUCTION
Bekah Thrasher

METRIC CONVERSION CHART		
to convert	*to*	*multiply by*
inches	centimeters	2.54
centimeters	inches	0.4
feet	centimeters	30.5
centimeters	feet	0.03
yard	meters	0.9
meters	yard	1.1

Acknowledgments

I'm so grateful to have been given the opportunity to write a knitting book for Interweave. It was a year ago that I received an email from Allison Korleski, then the editorial book director, asking to meet with me to discuss the idea of a book. By luck, when the email arrived, I was surrounded by family, enjoying an Indian lunch with my brother, sister, and husband, while on a family vacation in Colorado. After freaking out with those present, I immediately called my mom and dad to share the good news. Thank you, Allison, for this cherished memory and for giving me this amazing opportunity.

I would like to thank my family for believing in me, encouraging me, and being there for me when this opportunity occasionally became overwhelming. Mom, Dad, Jeff, Erin, Michael, Knansee, Susan, and Rainer: you guys are a fantastic support system. I love you so much. Most of all, I would like to thank my husband, also named Alex, who put up with long hours, a limited social calendar, and extra chores around the house. I'm pretty sure that if a marriage can survive the writing of a book, it can survive anything.

My friends have given me wonderful support. I would especially like to thank Rebecca, Brian, and Claire for being my sounding boards, offering awesome advice, and for Korean food Spa World dates when I needed a break.

Knitting has brought so many special people into my life. I really enjoyed the company of my fellow knitters and knitting students while I knitted the designs in this book. Their enthusiasm was contagious and kept me going when my fingers felt like they might fall off.

I will forever be indebted to Eunny Jang, who, when editor of *Interweave Knits*, took a chance on an unknown designer and accepted my first two published designs for the Fall 2012 issue of *Knits*—the Pluie Cardigan and the Woven Rain Hat. Thank you, Eunny, for giving me my start.

The staff at Interweave has been a pleasure to work with. Kerry Bogert expertly guided me through the proposal process, while also sharing some terrific gardening and baking tips along the way. Hollie Hill was instrumental in acquiring all of the yarn, keeping me updated with progress reports, and generally being awesome. My fantastic editor, Ann Budd, shared her vast knowledge of manuscript writing, and I was grateful to have clear and concise guidelines with which to work. Lori Gayle worked her tech-editing magic on my patterns, making sure that all the numbers add up, and Veronica Patterson made sure all of the i's are dotted and t's are crossed.

Thank you to ArtYarns, Berroco, Cascade, Knitting Fever, Malabrigo, MadelineTosh, Simply Shetland, Stonehinge Fiber Mill, and Westminster Fibers for generously providing all of the yarn you see on these pages.

Finally, I would like to thank all the knitters who are keeping my dream alive with their purchase of this book. I hope that it brings you hours of enjoyment and a sense of accomplishment when you wear your finished garments. Share them with me on Twitter and Instagram using @worldknits or #worldknits.

Table of Contents

The Ritual of Dressing

As a little girl, I remember the air of mystery that surrounded my mom as she got ready for her day—the careful selection of an outfit, the time spent getting her hair just so, applying the right shade of lipstick, and stepping into high heels. It was magical, and she looked beautiful. Now, as a woman, I share this ritual of dressing with my mother and her mother and the generations of women who came before.

In addition to a love of fashion, my mom fostered my interest in sewing. When I was little, she took me to the fabric store to select remnants that I would then use to create clothing for my American Girl doll, Samantha. My mom taught me the basics of handsewing and eventually let me use the sewing machine. As I got older, I transitioned from making clothing for Samantha to making clothing for myself. With my mom's encouragement, I grew more and more confident in my skills. This early experimenting led me to pursue patternmaking and construction later in the knitting world.

I learned to knit while in college, thankful to find a craft that was more portable than sewing. My first projects were painfully inept, misshapen, and full of mistakes, but I stuck with knitting and slowly improved. When my mom put my first copy of *Interweave Knits* in my Christmas stocking, I pored over it, excited by the possibility of no longer knitting rectangles. As I became comfortable knitting garments, I began taking risks and challenging myself to modify existing designs. Success with modifications eventually led me to design my own knitwear.

As a designer, I take pleasure in creating the pieces that make up my wardrobe. Drawn to slow fashion, I appreciate clothing that stands the test of time, both in quality and design. Handknits embody these ideals—carefully crafted in quality natural yarns, they can be passed down from mother to daughter, much like a cherished piece of jewelry. When sketching the designs for this book, I kept this ideal in the forefront of my mind.

Dressed in Knits is a collection of nineteen chic garments and accessories that are modern takes on classic feminine silhouettes. With looks that can be styled for the office, the weekend, or a night out, these timeless designs are refreshingly easy to wear. Five chapters of projects follow a foundation chapter, each set of projects inspired by an element in the ritual of dressing. I hope that you'll take pleasure in creating these luxe garments, from foundation pieces to outerwear and everything in between. And like the perfect shade of lipstick, the attention to detail and the couture finishing of these designs allows you to step out of the house with confidence.

Happy knitting!

Chapter 1

Knitting Foundations

Knitting garments that fit well depends on the right foundation. The finishing of a garment actually begins before you cast on a single stitch, and it continues with every choice you make until the last seam is sewn. If you take the time to put a little thought into each step along the way, you'll end up happy with the results.

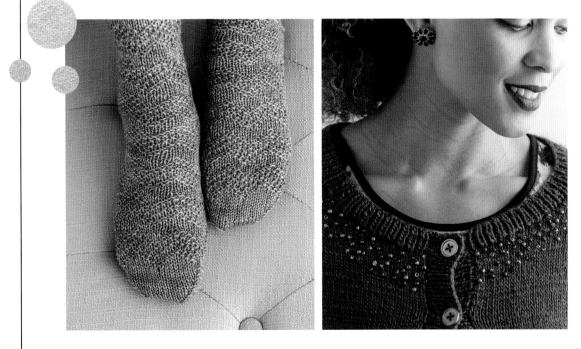

Before you cast on

The materials you select and the groundwork that you lay at the onset will affect your finished garment as much as when you join the pieces together.

Selecting Yarn

When you choose yarn for a project, it's important to select the best materials for the job. As I selected yarns for the designs in this book, I looked for fibers that provide ideal structure, drape, stitch definition, elasticity, function, seasonal wearabilty, and durability. I always suggest using natural fibers if you can afford them. They wear better than their synthetic counterparts, and they stand the test of time.

That said, I realize that knitters don't always use the yarn suggested in a pattern. If you do choose to make substitutions, keep in mind the weight and fiber content of the specified yarn. Different weights of yarn will affect the gauge, and different fibers may have characteristics that can lead to quite different effects (for a discussion on fibers and their characteristics, visit www.worldknits.com and search "substituting yarn").

For example, a mohair-nylon-wool blend at 230 yards (210 meters) per 50 grams should be a good substitute for a mohair-nylon blend at 115 yards (105 meters) per 25 grams because they have similar weights (both are 4.6 yards [4.2 meters] per gram) and similar fiber contents. A mohair-silk blend at 229 yards (209 meters) per 25 grams would

be less successful. The fiber content will provide similar drape, but the yarn is significantly thinner at 9.2 yards (8.4 meters) per gram. Although it's quite possible to substitute a different fiber or fiber blend, bear in mind that your piece may not drape or wear as well as it would made with the suggested yarn. Whenever you use a different yarn than specified in a pattern, even one that's similar in weight and fiber content, knit a swatch to ensure that you're happy with the drape or "hand" of the fabric at the gauge specified in the pattern.

The Importance of Gauge

Gauge is the measurement of the number of stitches and rows over a particular horizontal and vertical distance—typically 4 inches (10 centimeters). Although gauge is generally reported over 4 inches (10 centimeters) in the instructions, the magic number that designers use, and that you would use if you needed to modify a pattern, is the gauge over 1 inch (2.5 centimeters). But it's difficult to accurately measure gauge over such a short distance, particularly if partial stitches are involved. That's why gauge is typically measured over 4 inches (10 centimeters), then divided by four to get the number of stitches and rows in 1 inch (2.5 centimeters) of knitting.

For example, a gauge that's reported as 21 stitches and 28 rows to 4 inches (10 centimeters) translates to 5.25 stitches and 7 rows per inch (2.5 centimeters). It's easy to count the 21 stitches in a 4-inch (10-centimeter) width, but much more difficult to discern the difference between 5 and 5.25 (or 5.25 and 5.5) stitches in a single inch (2.5 centimeters). But that quarter of a stitch can add up to several inches when multiplied by the entire circumfer-

ence of a garment, and it can make the difference between a garment that fits just right and one that doesn't quite fit.

Before you begin any project, knit a gauge swatch. Cast on two more than the number of stitches specified for 4 inches (10 centimeters) to allow for a selvedge stitch on each side. Work in the specified pattern stitch until your piece measures a little more than 4 inches (10 centimeters) long.

A proper gauge swatch should be knitted, washed, and blocked just as you plan to knit, wash, and block the finished piece. After the swatch has dried, count the number of stitches and rows in the swatch and compare it to the specified gauge. If your numbers match the numbers listed, congratulations—you've gotten gauge, and you can start the project. If you have too many stitches, try again with larger needles; if you have too few stitches, try again with smaller needles. Repeat the process until you match the listed gauge.

In general, row gauge is not as important as stitch gauge, so if you can only get one of the two numbers, make sure it's the stitch gauge. Stitch gauge is key because patterns typically instruct you to work a certain number of inches (centimeters), not a specific number of rows. Exceptions to this approach include raglan and dolman pullovers and garments that have waist or bust shaping. In these cases, the row gauge is instrumental in positioning the shaping in the right places.

It's important to note that the gauge listed in the pattern is the gauge that the designer has instructed for the project and has little to do with the gauge specified on the ball band. Like all knitters, designers can be loose, tight, or spot-on when it comes to gauge. Even if you know that you're loose, tight, or spot-on, it's vital that you complete a gauge swatch to ensure that your gauge matches that of the designer. I understand it's frustrating and time-consuming to complete a gauge swatch, but it's far more frustrating to spend hours knitting only to end up with a garment that doesn't fit.

Getting the Right Fit

The first step in creating a garment that fits is to determine your measurements at key locations on your body. With the help of a friend, take the measurements listed below, then use these measurements (allowing for the desired amount of ease) when you select which size to knit.

1 *Bust:* Measure around the widest part of your bust.

2 *Waist:* Measure around the narrowest part of your waist.

3 *High Hip:* Measure around your hips at the top of your hip bones.

4 *Hip:* Measure around the widest part of your hips, between your high hip and crotch.

5 *Upper Arm:* Measure around the widest part of your upper arm.

6 *Forearm:* Measure around your forearm, where a three-quarter-length sleeve would hit.

7 *Cross Back Width:* Hold a knitting needle in each armpit and measure the horizontal distance between the two needles.

8 *Back-to-Waist Length:* Measure vertically from the top of your vertebrae to the narrowest part of your waist.

9 *Waist-to-Hip Length:* Measure vertically from the narrowest part of your waist to where you would like your garment to hit.

10 *Short-Sleeve Length:* Measure vertically from your armpit to midway down your upper arm.

11 *Three-Quarter-Sleeve Length:* Measure vertically from your armpit to midway down your forearm.

12 *Full-Sleeve Length:* Measure vertically from your armpit to your wrist.

Fill in your actual measurements in the table at right for future reference.

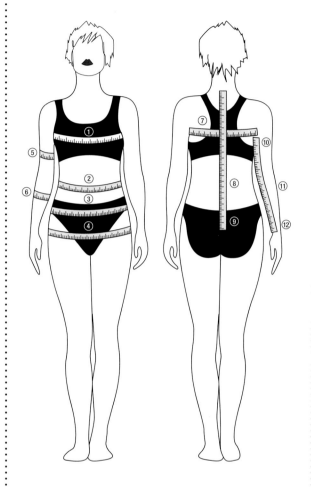

BUST CIRCUMFERENCE	
WAIST CIRCUMFERENCE	
HIGH HIP CIRCUMFERENCE	
HIP CIRCUMFERENCE	
UPPER ARM CIRCUMFERENCE	
FOREARM CIRCUMFERENCE	
CROSS BACK WIDTH	
BACK-TO-WAIST LENGTH	
WAIST-TO-HIP LENGTH	
SHORT-SLEEVE LENGTH	
THREE-QUARTER-SLEEVE LENGTH	
FULL-SLEEVE LENGTH	

Understanding Ease

Ease is the difference from your actual body measurements and the garment measurements. It's what allows you to move in your clothing. Knitted fabric differs from woven fabric in that it stretches in all directions, which means that knitwear requires less ease than woven wear. In fact, knitwear can have negative ease—a garment can be smaller than your actual body measurements—and still allow for comfortable movement.

In general, knitted garments range from very close fitting to loose fitting, depending on the amount of ease. I've included this information at the beginning of the instructions in this book so that you'll know my intentions for the fit of the garments. But if you're more comfortable with a different fit, choose a size that allows for the amount of ease that you prefer, based on the following guidelines.

Very Close Fitting: About 1 inch (2.5 centimeters) of negative ease; garment is smaller than your actual body measurements (think Mariah Carey dress).

Close Fitting: About 1 inch (2.5 centimeters) of positive ease; garment is roughly the same as your actual body measurements (think pencil skirt).

Standard Fitting: About 3 inches (7.5 centimeters) of positive ease; garment is moderately larger than your actual body measurements (think standard sweater).

Loose Fitting: About 6 inches (15 centimeters) of positive ease; garment is significantly larger than your actual body measurements (think sweatshirt).

As You Knit

Just as selecting the right materials and choosing the right fit are fundamental, the attention paid to details along the way is key to the overall success of a garment.

Casting On

Because the cast-on edge is often visible, choosing the right cast-on can make a difference in the appearance of your finished garment. If the cast-on edge is too tight, the fabric can pucker; if the cast-on edge is too loose, the fabric can look messy and uneven.

For the projects in this book, I've specified particular cast-ons when they're necessary for a particular look or function. Otherwise, I use the long-tail method (see Glossary). Visit www.worldknits.com for an instructional video. If you're interested in learning more ways to begin and end your projects, check out *Cast On, Bind Off* by Cap Sease (see Bibliography).

Blind Hem

When I want to avoid ribbing at the hem of a garment, one of my favorite techniques is the blind hem. It prevents stockinette-stitch fabric from rolling without interrupting the clean lines of the stitch pattern.

To work a blind hem, begin with a provisional cast-on (see Glossary), then work the facing for about 1 inch (2.5 centimeters), ending with a right-side row. Work a turning ridge on the next (wrong-side) row by knitting every stitch through the back loop to create a crisp edge. On the next (right-side) row, work the first row of the body pattern. To finish the hem, fold the fabric along the turning ridge to the wrong side and sew the live stitches in place.

Selvedges

To make easy work of seaming and picking up stitches, I like to use selvedge stitches for clean edges. My two favorites are slipped-stitch and garter-stitch selvedges.

A **slipped-stitch selvedge** is worked by slipping the first stitch purlwise (while holding the yarn in back) of every row, and working the last stitch as usual. This method creates a flat chain along the edge, which looks clean and neat on an unfinished edge. This type of selvedge is ideal for the heel flap on a sock because it identifies where to pick up stitches later on. However, I don't recommend this selvedge along a longer vertical edge because the elongated gap between stitches in a vertical column can lead to a messy-looking seam in the end.

A **garter-stitch selvedge** is worked by knitting the first and last stitch of every row. This method creates an easily identifiable column along which to seam or to pick up stitches along a long vertical edge, such as a button or buttonhole band.

Binding Off

When you bind off, it's important to maintain the same tension as in the knitted fabric and to be careful not to pull the yarn too tight. The bind-off edge should lie flat without puckering. My preferred method is the standard bind-off (see Glossary), but I will use a different bind-off if I feel that the fabric calls for it. For example, when binding off lace or anything that needs a loose edge, I will choose an inherently stretchier method, such as the sewn bind-off. For the projects in this book, use the standard bind-off unless I specify a different method.

Finishing Techniques

When you bind off the last stitch, the knitting may be complete, but the garment isn't finished. Loose ends need to be secured, seams need to be sewn, edgings need to be added, and the entire piece needs to be blocked. These are important steps for a professional look, and although they can be worked in different sequences, I've listed them below in my preferred order. Of course, not all garments will require all the steps.

- Weave in loose ends.
- Block (only lace or fabrics with uneven edges).
- Sew side seams.
- Sew shoulder seams.
- Sew sleeve seams.
- Sew sleeve caps into armholes.
- Sew hem, if necessary.
- Pick up stitches and knit neckband.
- Pick up stitches and knit buttonband.
- Pick up stitches and knit buttonhole band.
- Finish the zipper edge and attach zipper.
- Finish pockets and other embellishments.
- Block.

Note that unless I'm working with lace or a fabric that has wonky edges (such as the uneven edges produced by the tweed stitch in the Asciano Tweed Moto Jacket on page 124), I prefer to wait to block my garments until after they have been seamed. Otherwise, I've found that they often don't fit properly.

Let's take a closer look at each of the finishing steps.

Weave In Loose Ends

Always weave your ends in on the wrong side of the fabric, avoiding the cast-on or bind-off edges; work a couple of rows in from the edges instead. Thread the yarn end on a tapestry needle and weave the tail for 2 to 3 inches (5 to 7.5 centimeters) vertically along a column of knit stitches in ribbing or horizontally across purl bumps in other stitch patterns. If your yarn is slippery (such as one that contains silk, rayon, or bamboo), you may want to weave it in longer (and secure it with Fray Check) to ensure it doesn't work its way out.

Seams

I find seaming a garment incredibly satisfying—the way the seams pull themselves together to form a tidy column is magical to watch. Follow the tips and instructions here for professional results.

Before you begin, use locking stitch markers or safety pins to hold the two pieces together while you sew a seam. Begin by pinning the fabric at each end, then at the center, and finally place as many pins as needed between the ends and center—about one pin every 3 inches (7.5 centimeters). Remove the pins as you get to them.

Vertical Seams

Vertical seams, such as side and sleeve seams, are best sewn using a mattress stitch. Work with the right sides of the fabric facing you.

Leaving a 6-inch (15-centimeter) tail, thread the seaming yarn on a tapestry needle.

With the right sides facing outward (facing you), bring the tapestry needle from back to front under one bar between the two edge stitches on one piece, then under the corresponding bar plus the bar above it on the other piece (*Figure 1*). *Pick up the next two bars on the first piece (*Figure 2*), then the next two bars on the other (*Figure 3*).

Repeat from *, pulling the seaming yarn tight enough to cause the selvedge stitches to roll to the wrong side, ending by picking up the last bar or pair of bars on the first piece.

Horizontal Seams

Horizontal seams, such as shoulder seams, are best sewn using horizontal grafting. Work with the right sides of the fabric facing you.

Leaving a 6-inch (15-centimeter) tail, thread the seaming yarn on a tapestry needle.

Working from right to left into the stitches adjacent to the bind-off edges, bring the tapestry needle out at the center of the first stitch (i.e., go under just the first leg of the first stitch) on the bottom piece, then bring the needle in and out under both legs of the first stitch on the top piece (*Figure 1*). *Bring the threaded needle into the center of the same stitch it came out of, then out from the center of the adjacent stitch so that it travels under two legs (*Figure 2*) on the bottom piece. Bring the needle in and out under both legs of the next stitch on the upper piece (*Figure 3*).

Repeat from *, pulling the seaming yarn tight enough to cause the bind-off edges to roll to the wrong side, ending by bringing the needle under a single leg of the last stitch on the bottom piece.

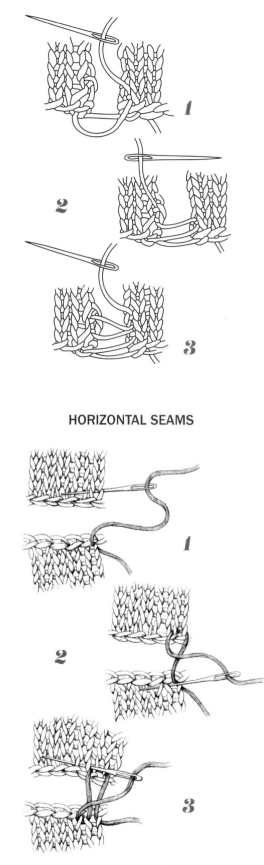

VERTICAL SEAMS

1

2

3

HORIZONTAL SEAMS

1

2

3

VERTICAL-TO-HORIZONTAL SEAMS

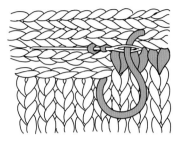

ALONG A HORIZONTAL EDGE

1

2

ALONG A VERTICAL OR SHAPED EDGE

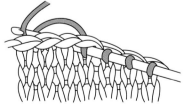

Vertical-to-Horizontal Seams

When it comes to sewing a sleeve cap into an armhole, use vertical-to-horizontal grafting, which is a combination of the vertical and horizontal seams already discussed.

Before you begin, use locking stitch markers or safety pins to position the sleeve cap properly in the armhole, matching the sleeve seam to the side seam at the base of the armhole, the center of the final cap bind-off row to the shoulder seam, and easing the fabric in between.

Leaving a 6-inch (15-centimeter) tail, thread the seaming yarn on a tapestry needle.

Begin at the base of the underarm, working upward to the shoulder seam, then back down to end at the base of the underarm, removing markers as you get to them.

*Bring the threaded needle from back to front in the center of a knit stitch just below the bind-off edge on the sleeve cap, under one or two bars between the first and second stitch in from the selvedge edge on the body, then under two legs of the next stitch under the bind-off edge.

Repeat from *, striving to match the tension of the knitting and pulling the seaming yarn tight to cause the edges to roll to the wrong side.

Picking Up Stitches

Buttonbands and collars are commonly finished by picking up stitches along the unfinished edges. The pattern will specify the number of stitches to pick up. Many knitters use the working knitting needle for picking up stitches but, if you're like me, you may find it much easier to use a crochet hook of the same size. Simply insert the hook through the fabric as instructed below to grab a loop onto the hook. Transfer the loops from the hook onto your knitting needle when the hook becomes too crowded with loops, being careful that the right leg of each loop is in front of the needle for proper stitch orientation, as shown in the illustrations at left.

To ensure an even distribution of picked up stitches, use locking stitch markers to divide the length of the pick-up edge into equal quarters. First, fold the piece in half to locate the midpoint of the edge to be picked up. Then, fold each end to the center and place another marker on each fold to divide the two halves into quarters. When picking up, plan to pick up one-fourth of the stitches in each section. For example, if the instructions say to pick up 84 stitches, pick up 21 in each quadrant.

Along a Horizontal Edge

When you pick up stitches along a horizontal edge (such as the center front neck or back neck edge of a neckband), pick up one stitch for every cast-on or bind-off stitch.

With right side facing and working from right to left, *insert the tip of the crochet hook into the center of the stitch below the bind-off or cast-on edge (*Figure 1*), wrap yarn around the hook, then pull through a loop (*Figure 2*).

Repeat from * for the desired number of stitches.

Along a Vertical or Shaped Edge

When you pick up stitches along a vertical or shaped edge (such as a buttonband or buttonhole band or along the sides of a neckband), you'll have to take into account the ratio of stitches to rows per inch (2.5 centimeters) of knitting. The goal is to pick up stitches at a rate that will result in a band that lies flat without puckers or gaps. The best way to determine the ratio of stitches to pick up is to practice on a swatch—your gauge swatch is ideal for this.

To begin, compare your stitch and row gauges. For example, if your gauge is 5 stitches and 7 rows to 1 inch (2.5 centimeters), you'll want to pick up 5 stitches for every 7 rows of knitting. To do this, pick up 1 stitch in each of the first 2 rows, skip 1 row, pick up 1 stitch in each of the next 3 rows, skip 1 row, then repeat the sequence. After you've worked a row or two, check to make sure that the band lies flat. If not, try again with a different ratio. If the band pulls in, pick up more stitches by skipping fewer rows; if the band ripples, pick up fewer stitches by skipping more rows. Don't be surprised if you have to stray from the number of stitches reported in the pattern to get the best-looking band.

With right side facing and working from right to left, insert hook between the last and second-to-last stitches, wrap the yarn around the hook, and pull through a loop. Pick up stitches according to the ratio of your stitch-to-row gauges, adjusting as necessary so that the picked-up edge lies flat.

Working Buttonbands and Buttonhole Bands

It's a good idea to work the buttonband first and mark the positions of the buttons on this band. Then work the buttonhole band, working buttonholes to correspond to the marked button positions. Typically, I position one button ½ inch (1.3 centimeters) up from the base of the band and one button ½ inch (1.3 centimeters) down from the top of the band. Then I fold the edge in half and place another button at the midpoint and all the others evenly spaced in between.

Buttonholes

At the appropriate row in the buttonhole band, work a buttonhole at each marked position. In general, a buttonhole should be a little smaller than the button. My preferred method is to work a yarnover followed by knitting two stitches together (yo, k2tog) for each buttonhole. It's easy to work and accommodates buttons that range from ¾ to ⅞ inch (2 to 2.2 centimeters) in diameter, when worked with DK-weight yarn (#3 Light). Another method that I like is worked over two rows. On the first row, work a ssk decrease, then a yarnover, then knit two stitches together (ssk, yo, k2tog), then on the following row, knit into the front and back of the yarnover. To accommodate larger buttons or yarn of a significantly different size, use Barbara Walker's one-row buttonhole technique, as explained in her *Second Treasury of Knitting* (see Bibliography).

Blocking

Blocking evens out stitches and helps the fabric blossom. When you work with lace, blocking opens the fabric to reveal the openwork pattern. Wet-blocking is the most involved method, followed by modified wet-blocking and steam-blocking.

Before you begin, check the yarn label to make sure it's okay for the yarn to get wet or to have heat applied to it. In general, you'll want to avoid heat on all synthetics, including rayon.

Wet-Blocking

Fill a basin with tepid water (I usually use my bathroom sink). If you want to clean the fabric as well, add a soap such as Soak, Eucalan, or any biodegradable dish soap.

Submerge the knitted piece(s), gently push out the air, then leave to soak for 10 minutes.

Remove from the water, gently squeezing out the excess water. Do not twist or wring knitted fabric, which can damage the fibers.

Place the wet piece(s) on a dry towel. Roll up the towel and press on it to draw out the remaining excess water.

Place the damp piece(s) on a flat surface (I use my carpeted floor; a bed or blocking mats also work well) and pin to measurements.

Allow to air-dry thoroughly before removing the pins.

Modified Wet-Blocking

Pin the piece(s) to measurements, then spritz with water until damp.

Allow to air-dry thoroughly before removing the pins.

Steam-Blocking

Lay the piece(s) flat on an ironing board, pinning in place if desired.

Hold a steam iron about 1 inch (2.5 centimeters) above the fabric (never touch the hot iron to the fabric) and blast it with a burst of steam.

Using your hands, gently flatten the fabric while it's damp from the steam.

For a heavier block, place a damp 100% cotton towel over the fabric and quickly press it with a hot iron.

Allow to air-dry thoroughly before removing the pins or moving from the ironing board.

Embellishments

Adding beads, sequins, or lace to your finished garment is an easy way to up the "wow" factor. It can also be a great way to draw the eye to a part of your body you may want to highlight. For example, if you're pear-shaped, you might want to add a visual element at the neckline to help to draw the viewer's eye to the top half of your body.

Beads or Sequins

Beads or sequins can be added onto stitches as you knit, or they can be sewn in place later. Because the yarn needs to be drawn through the hole in the bead or sequin to knit it in place, this type of application is typically restricted to laceweight or fingering-weight yarns. If you're using a heavier-weight yarn, you'll probably have the best luck if you sew the bead or sequin in place after the knitting has been completed. However the beads or sequins are added, keep the weight in mind. Many heavy beads can cause knitted fabric to stretch and distort.

Knitting Beads or Sequins into a Stitch

Knitting beads or sequins into a stitch is the most secure way to affix them to the knitted fabric, but placement is limited to individual stitches.

Work to the stitch designated for bead or sequin placement, knit the stitch, slip a bead or sequin onto the shaft of a small crochet hook, then use the crochet hook to slip the stitch just knitted from the right needle tip (*Figure 1*), slide the bead or sequin onto the stitch, then return the stitch to the right needle tip (*Figure 2*), adjusting the tension as necessary to match the other stitches.

Sewing Beads or Sequins onto Knitted Fabric

Sewing beads onto knitted fabric allows for infinite design possibilities. If the garment has positive ease, you can run sewing thread from bead to bead or sequin to sequin without worrying that the inelasticity of the sewing thread will restrict the garment's ability to stretch. But take care not to pull the thread too tightly between beads; doing so can distort the fabric. If, on the other hand, the garment has negative ease, use a separate length of sewing thread for each bead or sequin to ensure that the knitted stitches maintain their full ability to stretch.

Lace

Handknitted lace makes a striking embellishment, whether it's added to a handknitted (see the Montreal Lace Panel Cardigan on page 42) or store-bought garment. A bit of lace can add layered interest to any edge—be it the neck, front opening, cuff, or hem. You can save time by using commercial lace from your local fabric or thrift store. For the best results, apply the lace with a simple running-stitch seam (see Glossary) and tiny stitches in a coordinating color for an imperceptible seam.

KNITTING BEADS OR SEQUINS INTO A STITCH

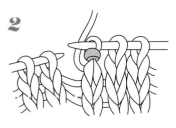

ZIPPERS

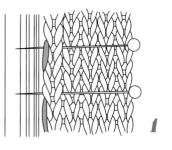

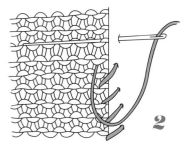

Zippers and Other Hardware

Adding zippers and other hardware to your knitting is a breeze when you follow the tips below.

Zippers

Zippers make excellent closures for handknits. Although zippers are ideal on dense fabrics or garments that are lined with woven fabric, don't discount them for lighter-weight or unlined knitted fabrics. If you're concerned about the zipper causing the knitting to stretch out of shape, reinforce the knitted edges with interfacing before adding the zipper.

Zippers are sold in a variety of lengths, colors, and teeth types. If you're unable to find just the right combination in your local fabric store, try an online source (see Sources of Supplies) for a custom zipper.

The two keys to a perfectly inserted zipper are having the same length of fabric on both sides and taking care not to stretch the knitting.

With right side facing and zipper closed, pin the zipper to the knitted pieces so that the edges meet at the zipper teeth. With contrasting thread, a sharp-point needle, and right side facing, baste the zipper in place close to the teeth (*Figure 1*) on both sides. Turn the work over and with matching sewing thread, stitch the outer edges of the zipper tape to the wrong side of the knitting (*Figure 2*), being careful to follow a single column of stitches in the knitting to keep the zipper straight. Turn the work again so that the right side is facing and use matching sewing thread and a backstitch seam (see Glossary) to sew the knitted fabric close to the teeth (*Figure 3*). Remove basting.

Grommets

Grommets are metal rings that reinforce holes made in fabric, securing the fabric's raw edges and producing a polished look (see the Laren Felted Cross-Body Bag on page 150). Grommets are available at most fabric stores and are surprisingly easy to insert—just follow the instructions that come with the hardware.

Grommets are best used on a knitted fabric that has been reinforced by small sewn stitches or felting. Simply mark the placement of the hole, then use the grommet tool to cut it out. With the right side facing, place the piece with the raised lip through the hole. Turn the fabric over so that the wrong side is facing and place the washer over the protruding grommet piece. Use the grommet tool to hammer the two pieces together.

Finishing Colorwork
. . . .

Steeks

Steeking is a technique that's commonly used in stranded-colorwork knitting so that the body can be worked completely in rounds from the hem to the neck—no need to work back and forth in rows, which can affect the tension in colorwork. Steeks are "extra stitches" added where the opening will occur. When the knitting is complete, the piece is cut along the center of the steek stitches and the raw edges are secured to the wrong side.

In general, steeks are best worked with "sticky" yarns, such as 100% wool. But if you follow these simple guidelines, you can rest assured that you can cut the fabric without the risk of stitches raveling.

Use smooth waste yarn in a contrasting color to baste a cutting line along the center of the steek stitches (*Figure 1*). Next, work a column of running stitches (as for a running-stitch seam; see Glossary) along each side of the center basting (*Figure 2*), followed by a line of backstitches (see Glossary) on top of the running stitches. Doing so will secure the knitting and prevent it from raveling. Finally, use a pair of sharp scissors to cut along the center basting line (*Figure 3*). Turn the cut edges to the wrong side and use whipstitch seams (see Glossary) to secure the facings in place.

Duplicate Stitches

Duplicate stitching is a lovely little technique that allows you to embroider knit stitches right onto the knitted fabric. In addition to embroidering motifs on plain stockinette stitch, you can also use duplicate stitches to correct misplaced colors in Fair Isle or intarsia patterns. I used duplicate stitches to turn the Falkirk Plaid Wrap (see page 154) striped fabric into a plaid. To ensure full coverage of the base stitches, be sure to use the same weight yarn for the duplicate stitches.

Bring the threaded tapestry needle up from the back at the base of the of the knit stitch to be covered, then insert it under both loops of the stitch in the row above it, and pull the needle through. For horizontal stitches, insert the needle into the base of the V again, and pull the needle through to the back of the work. For vertical stitches, bring the needle back out at the base of the stitch directly above the stitch just worked.

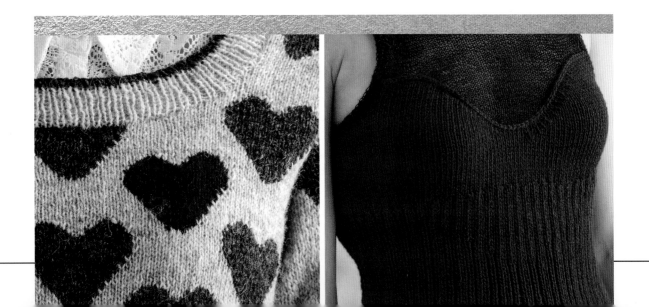

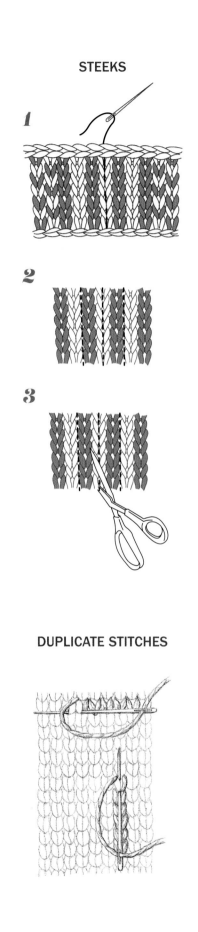

STEEKS

1

2

3

DUPLICATE STITCHES

Felting

Have you ever accidentally thrown a wool sweater in the wash only to find it half the size when it came out? Sadly, once wool shrinks, it will never be the same again. Sometimes in knitting, though, a shrunken, felted fabric is desirable. Felting transformed the Cabrillo Felted Boho Hat on page 146 from an oversize, sagging ugly duckling to a beautiful hat, giving it the structure necessary to its shape.

Felting produces a tight, water-resistant fabric and is achieved by agitating a piece of wool in hot, soapy water. Wool fibers are covered in little barbs that, when rubbed together under the influences of heat and moisture, cling to one another like Velcro (superwash wool will not felt because these barbs have been removed). Although most animal fibers will felt, I've found that wool gives me the best results.

The felting process is a continuum between light fulling, which causes the fibers to fluff and thicken, to full-on felting, which causes the fibers to lock onto one another and the fabric to shrink. The longer that you leave your fabric in the washer, the tighter the fibers will lock onto one another and the more the piece will shrink. To ensure that you're happy with the finished fabric, stop every few minutes to check the degree of felting.

If the felting is uneven, you may need to handfelt isolated areas—simply rub these areas under hot water.

Chapter 2

Foundation Garments

Getting ready in the morning shouldn't feel like a chore. To help start the day, I created a few garments that are luxurious to wear while you apply makeup and choose an outfit. The three designs in this chapter feature fabrics that feel divine against bare skin. Knitted from incredibly soft pima cotton, silk, alpaca, and merino wool, these knits will make you wish your morning routine took longer.

I like to keep a pair of socks handy on my nightstand so that when I climb out of bed in the morning, I have something warm to put on my feet. A pair of handknitted socks is luxury at its best. The *Visby Seeded Chevron Socks* (page 24), with their well-crafted heel cups and gusset shaping, hug feet in a way that store-bought socks cannot. Work them in a breathable natural fiber that you'll never want to take off your feet.

The *Tenerife Lace Camisole* (page 28), made with lustrous pima cotton, features a delicate lace border and thin garter-stitch straps. Lightweight and incredibly comfortable, it's perfect for a relaxing morning at home, but can also be paired with jeans or shorts for a day around town. Try tucking it into a linen or cotton skirt for a more polished look.

Finally, the *Gaborone Chemise-Inspired Dress* (page 34), based on a vintage chemise, hugs your body in all the right places. The delicate sheer alpaca fabric at the bust, mirrored in the ruffle at the hem, adds sexy allure to a dress that's comfortable enough for lounging around the house.

Visby

seeded chevron socks

Finished Size

About 7¼ (8½)" (18.5 [21.5] cm) foot circumference, 8½ (10)" (21.5 [25.5] cm) foot length from back of heel to tip of toe, and 9¾ (11¼)" (25 [28.5] cm) leg length from top of cuff to base of heel.

Socks shown measure 7¼" (18.5 cm) foot circumference.

Yarn

Fingering weight (#1 Super Fine).

Shown here: Madelinetosh Tosh Sock (100% superwash merino wool; 395 yd [361 m]/ 120 g): Heuchera (purple), 1 skein for each size.

Needles

Size U.S. 1 (2.25 mm): set of 5 double-pointed (dpn).

Adjust needle size if necessary to obtain the correct gauge.

Notions

Markers (m); stitch holder; tapestry needle.

Gauge

27½ sts and 36 rnds = 4" (10 cm) in St st worked in rnds.

25½ sts and 42½ rnds = 4" (10 cm) in seeded chevron patt from chart, worked in rnds.

Worked from the top down, these socks begin with a sturdy but flexible German twisted cast-on at the leg and end with a Kitchener-stitch toe. A seed-stitch element adds an unexpected bit of texture to a traditional chevron motif, one that's enhanced in the eye-of-partridge heel-flap pattern.

Refer to Chapter 1 for general knitting foundations.

Cuff Pattern (multiple of 10 sts, dec'd to multiple of 8 sts)

Rnds 1-7: *P1, [k1tbl, p1, k1tbl, k1] 2 times, k1tbl; rep from * to end.

Rnd 8: *P1, k1tbl, [p1, k1tbl, k2tog] 2 times; rep from * to end—patt has dec'd to a multiple of 8 sts.

Leg

Using the German twisted method (see Glossary), loosely CO 60 (70) sts. Arrange sts on 4 dpn so that there are 20 (22) sts each on Needles 1 and 3, and 10 (13) sts each on Needles 2 and 4.

Place marker (pm) and join for working in rnds, being careful not to twist sts.

Work Rnds 1–8 of Cuff patt (see Stitch Guide)—48 (56) sts rem after completing Rnd 8; piece measures about 1¼" (3.2 cm) from CO.

Rep Rnds 1–12 of Seeded Chevron Leg chart 6 (7) times—piece measures 8 (9¼)" (20.5 [23.5] cm) from

CO. To adjust leg length, work more or fewer 12-rnd patt reps; every 12 rnds added or removed will lengthen or shorten the leg by about 1¼" (3.2 cm).

Heel

Place last 24 (28) sts of rnd onto holder to work later for instep, then place first 24 (28) sts of rnd on a single dpn for heel.

Heel Flap

Work 24 (28) heel sts back and forth in rows as foll.

Row 1: (RS) *Sl 1 pwise with yarn in back (wyb), k1; rep from *.

Row 2: (WS) Sl 1 pwise with yarn in front (wyf), purl to end.

Row 3: Sl 2 pwise wyb, *k1, sl 1 pwise wyb; rep from * to last 2 sts, k2.

Row 4: Rep Row 2.

Rep these 4 rows 5 (6) more times, ending with Row 4—24 (28) total heel flap rows; 12 (14) chain sts at each selvedge; flap measures about 1¾ (2)" (4.5 [5] cm).

Turn Heel

Work short-rows to shape heel as foll.

☐ knit

• purl

☐ pattern repeat

SEEDED CHEVRON LEG

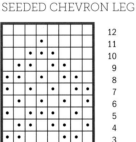

work 6 (7) times

SEEDED CHEVRON INSTEP

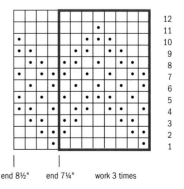

end 8½" end 7¼" work 3 times

Short-Row 1: (RS) Sl 1 pwise wyb, k13 (15), ssk, k1, turn work.

Short-Row 2: (WS) Sl 1 pwise wyf, p5, p2tog, p1, turn work.

Short-Row 3: Sl 1 pwise wyb, knit to 1 st before gap, ssk (1 st each side of gap), k1, turn work.

Short-Row 4: Sl 1 pwise wyf, purl to 1 st before gap, p2tog (1 st each side of gap), p1, turn work.

Rep Rows 3 and 4 until all sts have been worked, omitting the k1 or p1 after the dec in the last 2 rows—14 (16) heel sts rem.

Shape Gussets

Pick up sts along selvedge edges of heel flap and rejoin for working in the rnd as foll.

Set-up rnd: With a spare dpn, knit the first 7 (8) heel-flap sts; with Needle 1, k7 (8), then pick up and knit 13 (15) sts along side of heel flap. Return held instep sts onto needles with 12 (14) sts on each needle, and work Rnd 1 of Seeded Chevron Instep chart over these 24 (28) sts, ending as indicated for your size. With Needle 4, pick up and knit 13 (15) sts along other side of heel flap, then knit the first 7 (8) heel flap sts from spare dpn onto end of Needle 4—64 (74) sts total; 20 (23) sole sts each on Needles 1 and 4; 12 (14) instep sts each on Needles 2 and 3.

Rnd begs at center of sole.

Rnd 1: On Needle 1, knit to last 3 sts, k2tog, k1; on Needles 2 and 3, cont in patt; on Needle 4, k1, ssk, knit to end—2 sts dec'd; 1 st dec'd each from Needles 1 and 4.

Rnd 2: On Needle 1, knit; on Needles 2 and 3, work even in patt; on Needle 4, knit.

Rep the last 2 rnds 7 (8) more times—48 (56) sts rem; 12 (14) sts on each needle.

Foot

Cont even in patt as established until foot measures about 7¼ (8¼)" (18.5 [21] cm) from back of heel, or about 1¼ (1¾)" (3.2 [4.5] cm) less than desired total length.

Toe

Work in St st (knit every rnd) as foll.

Rnd 1: *On Needle 1, knit to last 3 sts, k2tog, k1; on Needle 2, k1, ssk, knit to end; rep from * for Needles 3 and 4—4 sts dec'd; 1 st dec'd from each needle.

Rnd 2: Knit.

Rep these 2 rnds 4 (6) more times—28 sts rem for both sizes.

Rep Rnd 1 (dec every rnd) 2 times—20 sts rem; 5 sts on each needle; toe measures about 1¼ (1¾)" (3.2 [4.5] cm) from last chart rnd.

Finishing

Knit the 5 sts from Needle 1 onto the end of Needle 4, then sl 5 sts from Needle 2 onto Needle 3—10 sts each on 2 needles.

Cut yarn, leaving a 20" (51 cm) tail. Use the Kitchener st (see Glossary) to graft sts tog.

Weave in loose ends.

Block as desired.

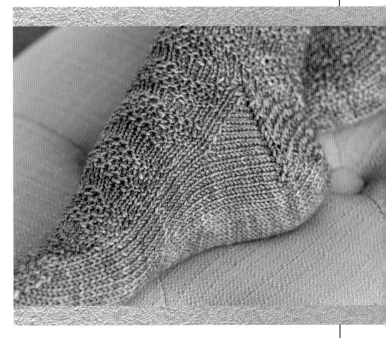

Tenerife

lace camisole

Finished Size

About 32¾ (36¾, 41, 45¼, 48¾, 52¾)"
(83 [93.5, 104, 115, 124, 134] cm) bust
circumference.

Designed to be worn with about 1" (2.5 cm) of
positive ease.

Camisole shown measures 32¾" (83 cm).

Yarn

Sportweight (#2 Fine).

Shown here: Cascade Ultra Pima Fine (100%
pima cotton; 136 yd [125 m]/50 g): #3719
Buff (beige), 5 (6, 6, 7, 7, 7) skeins.

Needles

Size U.S. 4 (3.5 mm): 24" to 40" (60 to
100 cm) circular (cir), depending on size.

*Adjust needle size if necessary to obtain the
correct gauge.*

Notions

Markers (m); smooth, contrasting waste yarn;
size E/4 (3.5 mm) crochet hook for provisional
CO; stitch holder; tapestry needle.

Gauge

23 sts and 28 rows/rnds = 4" (10 cm) in St st.

20 sts and 26 rows = 4" (10 cm) in lace patt
from Diamond chart.

Inspired by vintage camisoles, this
close-fitting version features a
hemmed lower edge and delicate lace
at the bust. It's worked in the round
to the armholes, then the front and
back are worked separately to the top
and finished with simple garter-stitch
edgings. The armhole edgings are
incorporated into matching garter-
stitch straps.

note

*Refer to Chapter 1 for general
knitting foundations.*

Body

With waste yarn, use the crochet provisional method (see Glossary) to CO 188 (212, 236, 260, 280, 304) sts. Change to main yarn. Place marker (pm) and join for working in rnds, being careful not to twist sts.

Work in St st (knit every rnd) until piece measures 1" (2.5 cm) from CO.

Hem fold line: Purl all sts through back loops (tbl).

Next rnd: K94 (106, 118, 130, 140, 152), pm for side "seam," knit to end.

Work even in St st until piece measures 14" (35.5 cm) from hem fold line for all sizes.

Dec rnd: Knit, dec 13 (13, 13, 19, 17, 17) sts evenly spaced across the next 94 (106, 118, 130, 140, 152) sts before first m, slip marker (sl m), knit to end—175 (199, 223, 241, 263, 287) sts rem: 81 (93, 105, 111, 123, 135) front sts, 94 (106, 118, 130, 140, 152) back sts.

Work garter eyelet band over front sts only as foll.

Rnd 1: Purl to m, sl m, knit to end.

Rnd 2: Knit all sts.

Rnd 3: Purl to m, sl m, knit to end.

Rnd 4: (eyelet rnd) K1, *yo, k2tog, rep from * to m, sl m, knit to end.

Rnd 5: Purl to m, sl m, knit to end.

Rnd 6: Knit all sts—piece measures 14¾" (37.5 cm) from fold line.

Front

Divide to work front and back separately in rows for your size as foll.

Sizes 32¾ (36¾, 45¼)" (83 [93.5, 115] cm) only
Next row: (RS) BO 4 (5, 7) sts, k1 (0, 1) so there are 2 (1, 2) st(s) on right needle after last BO, work Row 1 of Diamond chart over 69 (81, 93) sts, k6 (6, 9), remove m, place next 94 (106, 130) sts onto holder for back—77 (88, 104) front sts rem.

Next row: (WS) BO 4 (5, 7) sts, p1 (0, 1) so there are 2 (1, 2) st(s) on right needle after last BO, work Row 2 of Diamond chart over 69 (81, 93) sts, p2 (1, 2)—73 (83, 97) sts rem.

12¼ (12¾, 14, 15, 15¾, 15¾)"
31 (32.5, 35.5, 38, 40, 40) cm

3¼"
8.5 cm

4½"
11.5 cm

back and front

14¾"
37.5 cm

32¾ (36¾, 41, 45¼, 48¾, 52¾)"
83 (93.5, 104, 115, 124, 134) cm

Sizes 41 (48¾, 52¾)" (104 [124, 134] cm) only
Next row: (RS) BO 6 (9, 9) sts, then counting st on right needle after last BO as first chart st, work Row 1 of Diamond chart over 93 (105, 117) sts, k6 (9, 9), remove m, place next 118 (140, 152) sts onto holder for back—99 (114, 126) front sts rem.

Next row: (WS) BO 6 (9, 9) sts, then counting st on right needle after last BO as first chart st, work Row 2 of Diamond chart to end—93 (105, 117) sts rem.

Note: *During the following shaping, if there are not enough stitches at each side to work a decrease with its companion yarnover, work the stitches in stockinette instead. If there are not enough stitches to work a double decrease with both its yarnovers, work the stitches in stockinette, or substitute a yarnover and a single decrease if possible.*

All sizes
Working any sts outside of chart patt at each side in St st, work Rows 3–10 of chart and *at the same time* BO 2 (3, 3, 3, 5, 5) sts at beg of next 2 (2, 4, 4, 2, 2) rows, then BO 1 (2, 2, 2, 3, 4) st(s) at beg of next 6 (4, 4, 4, 4, 2) rows, then BO 0 (1, 0, 0, 2, 3) st(s) at beg of next 0 (2, 0, 0, 2, 4) rows—63 (67, 73, 77, 79, 87) sts rem.

Sizes 32¾ (36¾, 41, 45¼, 48¾)" (83 [93.5, 104, 115, 124, 134] cm) only
Next row: (RS) BO 1 st, purl to end—62 (66, 72, 76, 78) sts rem.

Next row: (WS) BO 1 st (1 st on right needle after BO), *p2tog, yo; rep from * to last 2 sts, p2—61 (65, 71, 75, 77) sts rem.

Size 52¾" (134 cm) only
Next row: (RS) BO 2 sts, purl to end—85 sts rem.

Next row: (WS) BO 2 sts (1 st on right needle after BO), *p2tog, yo; rep from * to last 2 sts, p2—83 sts rem.

Purling all sts every row, BO 2 sts at beg of next 2 rows, then BO 1 st at beg of foll 2 rows—77 sts rem.

All sizes
Purling all sts every row, work in garter st until armholes measure 2" (5 cm) for all sizes, ending with a WS row.

Shape Neck
With RS facing, p15 (16, 17, 18, 19, 19), join new ball of yarn and BO 31 (33, 37, 39, 39, 39) sts, purl to end—15 (16, 17, 18, 19, 19) sts rem each side.

	knit on RS; purl on WS
╱	k2tog
╲	ssk
⋀	sl 2 sts as if to k2tog, k1, p2sso
○	yo
	pattern repeat

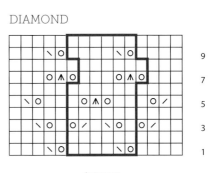

DIAMOND

6-st repeat

Working each side separately in established garter st (purl every row), at each neck edge BO 6 (6, 7, 7, 8, 8) sts once, then BO 4 (5, 5, 5, 5, 5) sts once, then BO 3 (3, 3, 4, 4, 4) once, then BO 2 sts once—no sts rem; armholes measure 3¼" (8.5 cm).

Back

Return 94 (106, 118, 130, 140, 152) held back sts to needle. Rejoin yarn with RS facing.

Shape Armholes
Working in St st (knit RS rows; purl WS rows), BO 6 (7, 8, 9, 11, 11) sts at the beg of the next 2 rows, then BO 2 (3, 3, 5, 5, 5) sts at the beg of the foll 2 (2, 4, 2, 2, 2) rows—78 (86, 90, 102, 108, 120) sts rem.

BO 1 (2, 2, 3, 3, 4) st(s) at the beg of the next 8 (4, 4, 2, 4, 2) rows, then BO 0 (1, 1, 2, 2, 3) st(s) at the beg of the foll 0 (4, 2, 4, 2, 4) rows—70 (74, 80, 88, 92, 100) sts rem.

BO 0 (0, 0, 1, 1, 2) st(s) at the beg of the next 0 (0, 0, 2, 2, 4) rows, then BO 0 (0, 0, 0, 0, 1) st at the beg of the foll 0 (0, 0, 0, 0, 2) rows—70 (74, 80, 86, 90, 90) sts rem.

Work even until armholes measure 3¼" (8.5 cm), ending with a WS row.

Shape Neck
With RS facing, k17 (18, 20, 21, 22, 22), join new ball of yarn and BO 36 (38, 40, 44, 46, 46) sts, knit to end—17 (18, 20, 21, 22, 22) sts rem each side.

Working each side separately in St st, at each neck edge BO 7 (7, 8, 9, 9, 9) sts once, then BO 5 (5, 6, 6, 6, 6) sts once, then BO 3 (4, 4, 4, 5, 5) sts once, then BO 2 sts once—no sts rem; armholes measure 4½" (11.5) cm.

Finishing

Block pieces to measurements.

Front Neckband
With RS facing, pick up and knit 61 (65, 71, 75, 77, 77) sts evenly spaced along front neck edge. Knit

3 rows, beg and ending with a WS row—2 garter ridges on RS.

BO all sts.

Back Neckband
With RS facing, pick up and knit 70 (74, 80, 86, 90, 90) sts evenly spaced across back neck edge. Knit 3 rows, beg and ending with a WS row—2 garter ridges on RS.

BO all sts.

Armhole Edgings and Straps
Notes: *Stitches for the straps are cast on between the stitches picked up along the front and back armhole edges. The cast-on numbers given produce armholes that measure 7 (7¾, 8¼, 9, 9¾, 9¾)" (18 [19.5, 21, 23, 25, 25] cm) high from base of underarm to shoulder line. To customize the armhole height, cast on more or fewer strap stitches; every 5 stitches added or removed will lengthen or shorten the strap by 1" (2.5) cm, which will increase or decrease the armhole height by ½" (1.3) cm.*

Left armhole and strap
With RS facing and beg at back neck edge, pick up and knit 40 sts along left back armhole to base of underarm, 24 sts along left front armhole to front neck edge, then use the backward-loop method (see Glossary) to CO 29 (35, 40, 46, 52, 52) sts—93 (99, 104, 110, 116, 116) sts total. Pm and join for working in rnds. Purl 1 rnd, knit 1 rnd, then purl 1 rnd—2 garter ridges on RS. BO all sts.

Right armhole and strap
With RS facing and beg at front neck edge, pick up and knit 24 sts along right-front armhole to base of underarm, 40 sts along right-back armhole to back neck edge, then use the backward-loop method to CO 29 (35, 40, 46, 52, 52) sts—93 (99, 104, 110, 116, 116) sts total. Pm and join for working in rnds. Purl 1 rnd, knit 1 rnd, then purl 1 rnd—2 garter ridges on RS. BO all sts.

Weave in loose ends.

Gaborone

chemise-inspired dress

Finished Size
About 33¼ (37¼, 41¼, 45¼, 49¼, 53¼)"
(84.5 [94.5, 105, 115, 125, 135.5] cm) bust
circumference; 24¾ (28, 32, 36¾, 40¾, 44¾)"
(63 [71, 81.5, 93.5, 103.5, 113.5] cm) waist
circumference.

Designed to be worn with about 1¼" (3.2 cm) of
positive ease at bust.

Dress shown measures 33¼" (84.5 cm) at bust.

Yarn
Worsted weight (#4 Medium) and Laceweight
(#0 Lace).

Shown here: Cascade Venezia Worsted (70%
merino wool, 30% mulberry silk; 219 yd
[200 m]/100 g): #180 Blue Mist (MC), 4 (4,
4, 5, 5, 5) skeins.

Cascade Alpaca Lace (100% baby alpaca;
437 yd [400 m]/50 g): #1401 Blue Mist (CC),
1 (2, 2, 2, 2, 2) skeins(s).

Needles
Body and strap edges: size U.S. 7 (4.5 mm) 24"
to 40" (60 to 100 cm) circular (cir) depending
on finished size.

Ruffle, ruching, and strap centers: size U.S. 4
(3.5 mm) 24" to 40" (60 to 100 cm) circular
(cir) depending on finished size.

Sheer bust: size U.S. 2 (3 mm) 24" to 40" (60 to
100 cm) circular (cir) depending on finished size.

I-cord trim: one size U.S. 7 (4.5 mm) double-pointed (dpn).

*Adjust needle size if necessary to obtain the
correct gauge.*

Notions
Markers (m); tapestry needle; 1¾ (2, 2¼, 2½,
2½, 2¾) yd (1.6 [1.8, 2.1, 2.3, 2.3, 2.5] meters)
of ¼" (6 mm) elastic; sharp-point sewing needle
and matching thread.

Sheer ruffled edges add feminine
allure to this close-fitting chemise-
style dress, which can be worn as
an underlayer or for comfortable
lounging. The dress is worked in
rounds from the bottom up, with hip
and bust shaping, as well as a ribbed
waist. I-cord trim accentuates the
bust, and a bit of elastic ensures a
body-hugging fit.

 *Refer to Chapter 1 for general
knitting foundations.*

Gauge
20 sts and 28 rnds = 4" (10 cm) in St st with
MC on largest needle.

28 sts and 36 rnds = 4" (10 cm) in St st with
CC on smallest needle.

Ruffle

With CC and middle-size needle, CO 384 (424, 464, 504, 544, 584) sts. Place marker (pm) and join for working in rnds, being careful not to twist sts.

Work in St st (knit every rnd) until piece measures 3" (7.5 cm) from CO with lower edge unrolled.

Body

Change to largest cir needle and MC.

Set-up rnd: *K2tog; rep from *—192 (212, 232, 252, 272, 292) sts rem.

Next rnd: K96 (106, 116, 126, 136, 146), pm for side "seam," knit to end.

Work even in St st until piece measures 1" (2.5 cm) from end of ruffle and 4" (10 cm) from CO.

Note: *To adjust length, work more or fewer rounds here; every 7 rounds added or removed will lengthen or shorten the dress by 1" (2.5 cm).*

Shape Hips

Dec rnd: *K1, k2tog, knit to 3 sts before m, ssk, k1; slip marker (sl m); rep from * once more— 4 sts dec'd.

Rep dec rnd every 8th rnd 5 more times, then every 6th rnd 4 (2, 2, 4, 4, 4) times, then every 4th rnd 7 (10, 10, 7, 7, 7) times—124 (140, 160, 184, 204, 224) sts rem.

Knit 1 rnd even—piece measures 17½" (44.5 cm) from CO.

Waist Ribbing

Next rnd: *[K1, p1] 7 (7, 9, 9, 11, 11) times, k34 (42, 44, 56, 58, 68), [p1, k1] 7 (7, 9, 9, 11, 11) times; sl m and rep from * once more.

Work in patt as established (knit the knits and purl the purls) until ribbed section measures 3½" (9 cm)—piece measures 21" (53.5 cm) from CO.

Shape Bust

Resume working all sts in St st, and cont as foll.

Inc rnd: *K1, M1 (see Glossary), knit to 1 st before m, M1, k1; sl m and rep from * once more—4 sts inc'd.

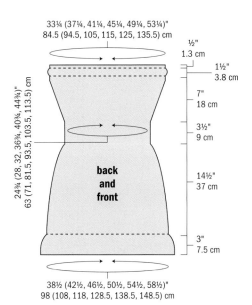

33¼ (37¼, 41¼, 45¼, 49¼, 53¼)"
84.5 (94.5, 105, 115, 125, 135.5) cm

½"
1.3 cm

1½"
3.8 cm

7"
18 cm

3½"
9 cm

14½"
37 cm

3"
7.5 cm

24¾ (28, 32, 36¾, 40¾, 44¾)"
63 (71, 81.5, 93.5, 103.5, 113.5) cm

back and front

38½ (42½, 46½, 50½, 54½, 58½)"
98 (108, 118, 128.5, 138.5, 148.5) cm

Rep inc rnd every 4th rnd 2 (4, 4, 2, 2, 2) more times, then every 6th rnd 1 (0, 0, 1, 1, 1) time(s), working new sts in St st—140 (160, 180, 200, 220, 240) sts.

Mark the last rnd completed for placement of I-cord underbust trim.

Change to CC and smallest needles.

Knit 1 rnd even.

Next rnd: Knit and *at the same time* inc 56 (64, 72, 80, 88, 96) sts evenly spaced—196 (224, 252, 280, 308, 336) sts.

Rep inc rnd, then [work 3 rnds even, rep inc rnd] 8 times—232 (260, 288, 316, 344, 372) sts.

Work even until piece measures 27½" (70 cm) from CO.

Change to MC and largest needles.

Next rnd: Knit and *at the same time* dec 66 (74, 82, 90, 98, 106) sts evenly spaced—166 (186, 206, 226, 246, 266) sts rem.

Purl 3 rnds—piece measures 28" (71 cm) from CO.

Ruching
Change to CC and middle-size needles.

Knit 1 rnd even.

Next rnd: *K1, M1; rep from *—332 (372, 412, 452, 492, 532) sts.

Work even in St st until ruching measures 1½" (3.8 cm)—piece measures 29½" (75 cm) from CO.

Upper Edge
Change to MC and largest needles.

Next rnd: *K2tog; rep from *—166 (186, 206, 226, 246, 266) sts rem.

Purl 3 rnds—piece measures 30" (76 cm) from CO.

BO all sts.

Finishing

Block to measurements, taking care not to flatten ruching.

Straps (Make 2)

With MC and largest needles, CO 60 (65, 65, 70, 70, 75) sts. Work 3 rows in Rev St st (purl RS rows; knit WS rows), beg and ending with a RS row.

Change to CC and middle-size needles.

Purl 1 WS row.

Next row: (RS) *K1, M1; rep from * to last st, k1—119 (129, 129, 139, 139, 149) sts.

Work even until CC section measures 1" (2.5 cm) from last MC row, ending with a RS row.

Next row: (WS) *P2tog; rep from * to last st, p1—60 (65, 65, 70, 70, 75) sts rem.

Change to MC and largest needles. Work 3 rows in Rev St st, beg and ending with a RS row.

BO all sts.

If desired, block straps to 12 (13, 13, 14, 14, 15)" (30.5 [33, 33, 35.5, 35.5, 38] cm) wide and about 1½" (3.8 cm) high with Rev St st edges at top and bottom allowed to roll to WS, and taking care not to flatten center of straps.

Lay dress flat with side "seams" aligned with side folds. With MC threaded on a tapestry needle, sew straps to upper edge of dress, leaving 7 (7, 7½, 7½, 8, 8)" (18 [18, 19, 19, 20.5, 20.5] cm) between straps at center front and back.

I-Cord Trim

Work applied I-cord along the underbust where the fabric transitions from solid MC to sheer CC as foll.

With RS facing, beg and ending at left side "seam," slip a cir needle into the sts of the marked MC rnd (last rnd below sheer bust section); these sts are just placed on the needle, not picked up and knitted—140 (160, 180, 200, 220, 240) sts. With MC and dpn, CO 3 sts.

With RS facing and beg at left side "seam," *slide 3 I-cord sts to beg of dpn, k2, sl last I-cord st pwise with yarn in back, yo, knit first st on cir needle, pass yo and slipped st over knit st—3 I-cord sts on dpn; 1 st from cir needle has been joined. Rep from * until all sts on cir needle have been joined. BO rem 3 I-cord sts. Sew ends of I-cord tog.

Weave in loose ends.

Elastic

Cut two pieces of elastic, each 31 (35, 39, 43, 47, 51)" (78.5 [89, 99, 109, 119.5, 129.5] cm) long. Overlap the ends of each piece by a small amount, being careful not to twist, and sew elastic into a ring using sharp-point sewing needle and matching thread. Using sewing needle and thread, sew elastic rings to WS of dress, with one centered on the 3 purl rnds below the ruching, and the other centered on the 3 purl rnds of the upper edge.

Chapter 3

Day

When designing for daytime, I was drawn to pieces that could easily be incorporated into a work wardrobe but that would be equally comfortable for the weekend. A natural fit was the cardigan. Belted, buttoned, or worn open, cardigans can change the look of an outfit with ease. Whether you're pairing a cardigan with a skirt, a dress, or pants, it offers the perfect knitted layer for trans-seasonal dressing.

The *Montreal Lace Panel Cardigan* and the *Bukhara Silk Brocade Cardigan* (pages 42 and 50, respectively) feature yarns that have bit of sheen. They look fantastic paired with richer fabrics, such as silks and polished cottons, but also look great with jeans and a white T-shirt. The attractive lace details on the Montreal and the beads on the Bukhara make for interesting knitting and set these cardigans apart from the ordinary.

I love the versatility of the *Aswan Dress with Tunic Option* (page 58). Initially designed to be worn with a nude slip, much like the dresses of the 1930s and 1940s, the Aswan, I was happy to discover, also looks great worn as a belted cardigan over a shift dress. The contrasting colored edging creates a bold visual line against the sheer nude fabric. For added versatility, I included patterns for two lengths—a longer dress length and a shorter tunic length.

The *Madingley Shawl-Neck Cardigan* (page 66) and the *Montmartre Intarsia Scoop-Neck Pullover* (page 74) feature more rustic fabrics and comfortable shapes. I envisioned these sweaters being worn on a weekend in front of a cozy fire or at a local coffee shop while knitting. The deep U-neck and relaxed fit make the Montmartre an easy sweater to pull on over button-up shirts; the casual pocket, elbow-patch details, and the wide shawl collar give the Madingley the comfort of an old friend.

Montreal
lace panel cardigan

Finished Size
About 34½ (38¾, 43, 47¼, 51, 55¾)" (87.5 [98.5, 109, 120, 129.5, 141.5] cm) bust circumference, including 1" (2.5 cm) front band.

Designed to be worn with 2½" (6.5 cm) to 3" (7.5 cm) of positive ease.

Cardigan shown measures 34½" (87.5 cm).

Yarn
DK weight (#3 Light) and fingering weight (#1 Super Fine).

Shown here: Madelinetosh Tosh DK (100% superwash merino wool; 225 yd [206 m]/100 g): Smokestack (MC, gray), 5 (6, 6, 7, 8, 8) skeins.

Madelinetosh Tosh Sock (100% superwash merino wool; 395 yd [361 m]/120 g): Stovepipe (CC, dark blue), 1 skein for all sizes.

Needles
Body and sleeves: size U.S. 6 (4 mm) 24" to 40" (60 to 100 cm) circular (cir) depending on garment size.

Ribbing: size U.S. 4 (3.5 mm) 24" to 40" (60 to 100 cm) cir depending on garment size.

Lace appliqués: size U.S. 1 (2.25 mm) straight.

Adjust needle size if necessary to obtain the correct gauge.

Notions
Stitch holder; tapestry needle; removable markers; seven ¾" (2 cm) buttons; sharp-point sewing needle; sewing thread to match CC.

Gauge
22 sts and 28 rows = 4" (10 cm) in St st with MC on largest needle.

24 sts at widest point of Chart A or C measure 3½" (9 cm) wide with CC on smallest needles, blocked.

40 rows (four 10-row reps) of Chart A or C measure 6" (15 cm) high with CC on smallest needles, blocked.

Contrasting lace panels transform a simple cardigan into a chic fashion statement. The base cardigan is worked flat in pieces that are seamed together. The lace panels are worked separately, then sewn in place along the front neck and openings. Coordinating buttons bring it all together.

Each repeat of lace Charts A and C begins with 19 stitches, increases to a maximum of 24 stitches, then decreases back to 19 stitches again.

Each repeat of lace Charts B and D begins with 6 stitches, increases to a maximum of 10 stitches, then decreases back to 6 stitches again.

Refer to Chapter 1 for general knitting foundations.

Back

With MC and middle-size needle, CO 106 (118, 130, 142, 154, 166) sts.

Next row: *K1, p1; rep from *.

Rep the last row for k1, p1 rib until piece measures 1" (2.5 cm), ending with a WS row.

Change to largest needle and St st.

Next row: Knit and *at the same time* dec 10 (10, 12, 12, 14, 14) sts evenly spaced—96 (108, 118, 130, 140, 152) sts rem.

Work even until piece measures 14½" (37 cm) from CO for all sizes, ending with a WS row.

Shape Armholes

BO 5 (5, 5, 8, 8, 8) sts at the beg of the next 2 rows, then BO 3 (3, 4, 5, 5, 5) sts at the beg of the foll 2 (4, 2, 2, 2, 2) rows—80 (86, 100, 104, 114, 126) sts rem.

BO 2 (2, 3, 3, 4, 4) sts at the beg of the next 4 rows, then BO 1 (1, 2, 2, 2, 3) st(s) at the beg of the foll 2 rows—70 (76, 84, 88, 94, 104) sts rem.

BO 0 (0, 1, 1, 1, 2) st(s) at the beg of the next 2 rows, then BO 0 (0, 0, 0, 0, 1) st at the beg of the foll 2 rows—70 (76, 82, 86, 92, 98) sts rem.

Work even until armholes measure 7 (7½, 8, 8½, 9, 9½)" (18 [19, 20.5, 21.5, 23, 24] cm), ending with a WS row.

Shape Neck and Shoulders

BO 3 (4, 4, 4, 5, 6) sts at the beg of the next 2 rows—64 (68, 74, 78, 82, 86) sts rem.

Next row: (RS) BO 3 (4, 4, 5, 5, 6) sts, knit until there are 18 (19, 21, 22, 23, 24) sts on right needle after BO, join new ball of yarn and BO 22 (22, 24, 24, 26, 26) center sts, knit to end—18 (19, 21, 22, 23, 24) sts rem for right shoulder; 21 (23, 25, 27, 28, 30) sts rem for left shoulder.

Place right shoulder sts onto holder.

Left Shoulder

Cont on 21 (23, 25, 27, 28, 30) left shoulder sts as foll.

Next row: (WS) BO 3 (4, 4, 5, 5, 6) sts, purl to end—18 (19, 21, 22, 23, 24) sts rem.

Next row: (RS) BO 6 sts at neck edge, knit to end—12 (13, 15, 16, 17, 18) sts rem.

Next row: BO 3 (4, 4, 5, 5, 6) sts, purl to end—9 (9, 11, 11, 12, 12) sts rem.

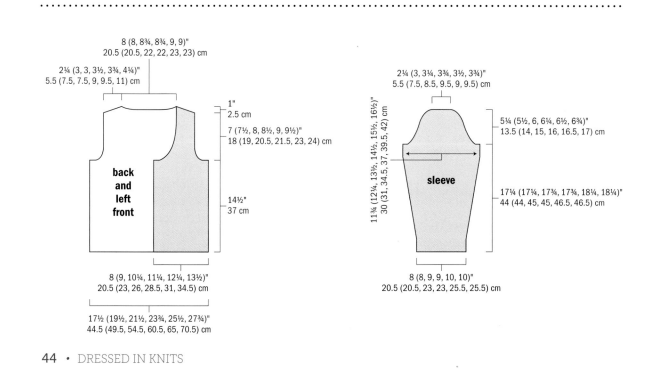

8 (8, 8¾, 8¾, 9, 9)"
20.5 (20.5, 22, 22, 23, 23) cm

2¼ (3, 3, 3½, 3¾, 4¼)"
5.5 (7.5, 7.5, 9, 9.5, 11) cm

1"
2.5 cm

7 (7½, 8, 8½, 9, 9½)"
18 (19, 20.5, 21.5, 23, 24) cm

back and left front

14½"
37 cm

8 (9, 10¼, 11¼, 12¼, 13½)"
20.5 (23, 26, 28.5, 31, 34.5) cm

17½ (19½, 21½, 23¾, 25½, 27¾)"
44.5 (49.5, 54.5, 60.5, 65, 70.5) cm

2¼ (3, 3¼, 3¾, 3½, 3¾)"
5.5 (7.5, 8.5, 9.5, 9, 9.5) cm

5¼ (5½, 6, 6¼, 6½, 6¾)"
13.5 (14, 15, 16, 16.5, 17) cm

11¾ (12¼, 13½, 14½, 15½, 16½)"
30 (31, 34.5, 37, 39.5, 42) cm

sleeve

17¼ (17¼, 17¾, 17¾, 18¼, 18¼)"
44 (44, 45, 45, 46.5, 46.5) cm

8 (8, 9, 9, 10, 10)"
20.5 (20.5, 23, 23, 25.5, 25.5) cm

Next row: BO 5 (5, 6, 6, 6, 6) sts at neck edge, knit to end—4 (4, 5, 5, 6, 6) sts rem.

BO all sts.

Right Shoulder

Return 18 (19, 21, 22, 23, 24) held right shoulder sts onto largest needle.

Next row: (WS) BO 6 sts at neck edge, purl to end—12 (13, 15, 16, 17, 18) sts rem.

Next row: (RS) BO 3 (4, 4, 5, 5, 6) sts, knit to end—9 (9, 11, 11, 12, 12) sts rem.

Next row: BO 5 (5, 6, 6, 6, 6) sts at neck edge, purl to end—4 (4, 5, 5, 6, 6) sts rem.

BO all sts.

Left Front

With MC and middle-size needle, CO 50 (56, 62, 68, 74, 80) sts.

Work in k1, p1 rib as for back until piece measures 1" (2.5 cm) from CO, ending with a WS row. Change to largest needle and St st.

Next row: (RS) Knit and *at the same time* dec 6 sts evenly spaced—44 (50, 56, 62, 68, 74) sts rem.

Work even until piece measures 14½" (37 cm) from CO, ending with a WS row.

Shape Armhole and Neck

Note: *Armhole and neck are shaped at the same time; read all the way through the foll section before proceeding.*

At armhole edge (beg of RS rows), BO 5 (5, 5, 8, 8, 8) sts once, then BO 3 (3, 4, 5, 5, 5) sts 1 (2, 1, 1, 1, 1) time(s), then BO 2 (2, 3, 3, 4, 4) sts 2 times, then BO 1 (1, 2, 2, 2, 3) st(s) once, then BO 0 (0, 1, 1, 1, 2) st(s) 0 (0, 1, 1, 1, 1) time, then BO 0 (0, 0, 0, 0, 1) st 0 (0, 0, 0, 0, 1) time—13 (16, 18, 22, 24, 27) sts total removed at armhole edge. *At the same time*, at the beg of WS rows, BO 6 (6, 7, 7, 8, 8) sts once, then BO 3 (3, 4, 4, 4, 4) sts 1 (1, 1, 1, 2, 2) time(s), then BO 2 (2, 3, 3, 2, 2) sts 3 (3, 1, 1, 2, 2) time(s), then BO 1 (1, 2, 2, 1, 1) st(s) 3 (3, 2, 2, 3, 3) time(s), then BO 0 (0, 1, 1, 0, 0) st 0 (0, 3, 3, 0, 0) times—18 (18, 21, 21, 23, 23) sts total removed

at neck edge; 13 (16, 17, 19, 21, 24) sts rem when all armhole and neck shaping is complete.

Work even until armhole measures 7 (7½, 8, 8½, 9, 9½)" (18 [19, 20.5, 21.5, 23, 24] cm), ending with a WS row.

Shape Shoulder

At armhole edge (beg of RS rows), BO 3 (4, 4, 4, 5, 6) sts once, then BO 3 (4, 4, 5, 5, 6) sts 2 times, then BO 4 (4, 5, 5, 6, 6) sts once—no sts rem.

Right Front

With MC and middle-size needle, CO 50 (56, 62, 68, 74, 80) sts.

Work in k1, p1 rib as for back until piece measures 1" (2.5 cm) from CO, ending with a WS row. Change to largest needle and St st.

Next row: (RS) Knit and *at the same time* dec 6 sts evenly spaced—44 (50, 56, 62, 68, 74) sts rem.

Work even until piece measures 14½" (37 cm) from CO, ending with a RS row.

Shape Armhole and Neck

Note: *Armhole and neck are shaped at the same time; read all the way through the foll section before proceeding.*

At armhole edge (beg of WS rows), BO 5 (5, 5, 8, 8, 8) sts once, then BO 3 (3, 4, 5, 5, 5) sts 1 (2, 1, 1, 1, 1) time(s), then BO 2 (2, 3, 3, 4, 4) sts 2 times, then BO 1 (1, 2, 2, 2, 3) st(s) once, then BO 0 (0, 1, 1, 1, 2) st(s) 0 (0, 1, 1, 1, 1) time, then BO 0 (0, 0, 0, 0, 1) st 0 (0, 0, 0, 0, 1) time—13 (16, 18, 22, 24, 27) sts total removed at armhole edge. *At the same time*, at the beg of RS rows, BO 6 (6, 7, 7, 8, 8) sts once, then BO 3 (3, 4, 4, 4, 4) sts 1 (1, 1, 1, 2, 2) time(s), then BO 2 (2, 3, 3, 2, 2) sts 3 (3, 1, 1, 2, 2) time(s), then BO 1 (1, 2, 2, 1, 1) st(s) 3 (3, 2, 2, 3, 3) time(s), then BO 0 (0, 1, 1, 0, 0) st 0 (0, 3, 3, 0, 0) times—18 (18, 21, 21, 23, 23) sts total removed at neck edge; 13 (16, 17, 19, 21, 24) sts rem when all armhole and neck shaping is complete.

Work even until armhole measures 7 (7½, 8, 8½, 9, 9½)" (18 [19, 20.5, 21.5, 23, 24] cm), ending with a RS row.

Shape Shoulder

At armhole edge (beg of WS rows), BO 3 (4, 4, 4, 5, 6) sts once, then BO 3 (4, 4, 5, 5, 6) sts 2 times, then BO 4 (4, 5, 5, 6, 6) sts once—no sts rem.

Sleeves

With MC and middle-size needle, CO 48 (48, 54, 54, 60, 60) sts.

Work in k1, p1 rib as for back until piece measures 1" (2.5 cm) from CO, ending with a WS row.

Change to largest needle and St st.

Next row: Knit and *at the same time* dec 4 (4, 4, 4, 5, 5) sts evenly spaced—44 (44, 50, 50, 55, 55) sts rem.

Work even until piece measures 2" (5 cm) from CO, ending with a WS row.

Inc row: K1, M1 (see Glossary), knit to last st, M1, k1—2 sts inc'd.

Rep inc row every 10 (8, 8, 8, 8, 6)th row 9 (11, 11, 3, 4, 14) times, then every 0 (0, 0, 6, 6, 4)th row 0 (0, 0, 11, 10, 3) times, working new sts in St st—64 (68, 74, 80, 85, 91) sts.

Work even until sleeve measures 17¼ (17¼, 17¾, 17¾, 18¼, 18¼)" (44 [44, 45, 45, 46.5, 46.5] cm) from CO, ending with a WS row.

Shape Cap

BO 5 (5, 5, 8, 8, 8) sts at the beg of the next 2 rows, then BO 2 sts at beg of next 4 (4, 4, 4, 4, 6) rows—46 (50, 56, 56, 61, 63) sts rem.

[BO 1 st at beg of next 2 rows, then work 2 rows even] 1 (2, 2, 4, 2, 2) time(s)—44 (46, 52, 48, 57, 59) sts.

BO 1 st at beg of next 22 (20, 24, 18, 28, 28) rows—22 (26, 28, 30, 29, 31) sts.

BO 2 sts at the beg of the next 2 rows, then BO 3 sts at the beg of the foll 2 rows—12 (16, 18, 20, 19, 21) sts rem.

BO all sts.

Lace Appliqués

Left Front

With CC, smallest needles, and using the German twisted method (see Glossary), CO 19 sts.

Purl 1 (WS) row.

Work Rows 1–10 of Chart A 8 times, then work Rows 1–9 once more (see Notes)—19 sts.

Next row: (WS) BO 13 sts, purl to end—6 sts rem.

Work Rows 1–8 of Chart B 6 (7, 8, 8, 9, 9) times (see Notes).

BO all sts as foll: K2, *insert left needle tip from left to right into the fronts of 2 sts on right needle tip, k2tog through back loop (tbl), k1; rep from * until 1 st rem.

Fasten off last st.

Right Front

With CC, smallest needles, and using the German twisted method, CO 19 sts.

Purl 1 (WS) row.

Work Rows 1–10 of Chart C 8 times, then work Rows 1–8 once more—24 sts.

Next row: (RS) BO 13 sts, knit to end—11 sts rem.

Next row: (WS) BO 5 sts, purl to end—6 sts rem.

Work Rows 1–8 of Chart D 6 (7, 8, 8, 9, 9) times.

BO all sts as for left front appliqué.

Weave in loose ends. Block each piece so that the Chart A or C section measures about 3½" (9 cm) wide at tips of points and 13½" (34.5 cm) along straight edge. Block the Chart B or D section to about 1¼" (3.2 cm) wide at tips of points and long enough to fit along the neck edge to the shoulder seam.

Finishing

Block body and sleeves to measurements. With yarn threaded on a tapestry needle, sew side seams. Sew shoulder seams. Sew sleeve seams. Sew sleeve caps into armholes, matching center of cap BO with shoulder seam, and matching sleeve seam with side seam at underarm.

CHART A, Left Front   CHART B, Left Front

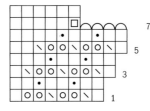

	knit on RS; purl on WS			yo
•	purl on RS; knit on WS		⌒	BO 1 st
/	k2tog on RS; p2tog on WS		□	st on right needle after last BO
\	ssk on RS; p2togtbl on WS			

Neckband

With MC, middle-size needle, and RS facing, pick up and knit 54 (58, 64, 68, 74, 78) sts evenly spaced along right front neck edge, 44 (44, 48, 48, 50, 50) sts evenly spaced across back neck edge, and 54 (58, 64, 68, 74, 78) sts evenly spaced along left front neck edge—152 (160, 176, 184, 198, 206) sts total.

Work in k1, p1 rib until piece measures 1" (2.5 cm) from pick-up row.

BO all sts in patt.

Buttonband

With MC, middle-size needle, and RS facing, pick up and knit 88 sts evenly spaced along left front edge. Work in k1, p1 rib until piece measures 1" (2.5 cm) from pick-up row

BO all sts in patt.

Mark placement of 7 buttons, with one ½" (1.3 cm) down from neck edge of band, one ½" (1.3 cm) up from bottom of band, and the others evenly spaced in between.

Buttonhole Band

With MC, middle-size needle, and RS facing, pick up and knit 88 sts evenly spaced along right front edge. Work in k1, p1 rib for 2 rows.

Next row: (WS) Work in rib, working a [yo, p2tog] buttonhole opposite each marked position on buttonband.

Cont in rib patt until band measures 1" (2.5 cm) from pick-up row.

BO all sts in patt.

Weave in loose ends.

Pin lace appliqués to cardigan fronts as shown in photographs. With sharp-point needle and matching thread, sew all the way around the perimeter of each piece, then tack the appliqués in place with vertical lines of stitches concealed in the vertical elements of the lace fabric.

Sew buttons to buttonband opposite buttonholes.

CHART C, Right Front

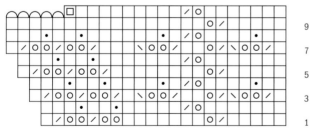

CHART D, Right Front

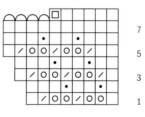

Bukhara

silk brocade cardigan

Finished Size

About 35 (39, 43¼, 47, 51¼, 55)" (89 [99, 110, 119.5, 130, 139.5] cm) bust circumference, including 1" (2.5 cm) front band.

Designed to be worn with 3" (7.5 cm) of positive ease.

Cardigan shown measures 35 (89 cm).

Yarn

Sportweight (#2 Fine) and laceweight (#0 Lace).

Shown here: Louisa Harding Grace Silk & Wool (50% merino wool, 50% silk; 110 yd [100 m]/ 50 g): #42 Russet (MC), 8 (9, 10, 11, 12, 13) balls.

Artyarns Silk Essence (100% silk; 400 yd [365 m]/45 g): #263 (CC, rust), 1 skein for all sizes.

Needles

Body and sleeves: size U.S. 7 (4.5 mm) 24" to 40" (60 to 100 cm) circular (cir) depending on finished size.

Lace borders: size U.S. 1 (2.25 mm) straight or 24" to 40" (60 to 100 cm) cir depending on finished size.

Adjust needle size if necessary to obtain the correct gauge.

Notions

Markers (m); stitch holders; about 30 (35, 40, 45, 50, 55) grams size 6/0 seed beads in an assortment of metallic-lined, crystal, and matte finishes to coordinate with MC; size 12 (1.0 mm) steel crochet hook (or size to fit through holes in beads); seven ¾" (2 cm) buttons; sharp-point sewing needle; sewing thread to match MC.

Gauge

22 sts and 30 rows = 4" (10 cm) in St st with MC on larger needle.

25 sts and 42 rows = 4" (10 cm) in lace patt from Bukhara charts with CC on smaller needles, blocked.

Beaded silk brocade detail gives this standard-fitting cardigan an upscale look that's great for office or weekend wear. The sweater is worked in pieces from the lower edges, beginning with rounded I-cord cast-ons that are followed by a wide band of delicate diamond brocade punctuated with beads. The detail is repeated around the sleeve cuffs while the wide neck opening is sprinkled with beads.

In the cardigan shown, the knitted-in beads of the lace borders are all the same color and style. The sewn-on beads at the neck are a mix of different colors and styles applied randomly.

Refer to Chapter 1 for general knitting foundations.

I-cord CO: Using the long-tail method (see Glossary), CO 3 sts. With RS facing, transfer sts to left needle, then bring yarn around behind the work, in position to work the first st on left needle. K1f&b (see Glossary), knit last 2 I-cord sts—4 sts: 3 I-cord sts and 1 CO st. *With RS facing, slip 3 sts purlwise with yarn in back from right needle to left needle, bring yarn behind the work, k1f&b, k2—3 I-cord sts and 1 new CO st added. Rep from * until the desired number of sts is on the right needle.

Place bead: Knit the stitch designated for a bead, slip a bead onto the shaft of a small crochet hook, then use the crochet hook to slip the stitch just knitted from the right needle tip, slide the bead onto the stitch, then return the stitch to the right needle tip, adjusting the tension as necessary to match the other stitches (see page 18).

Back

With CC, smaller needles, and using the I-cord method (see Stitch Guide), CO 127 (141, 155, 171, 185, 199) sts.

Next row: (WS) Purl and *at the same time* dec 16 (18, 20, 24, 26, 28) sts evenly spaced—111 (123, 135, 147, 159, 171) sts rem.

Work Rows 1–12 of Bukhara Chart A (see page 54) 2 times, ending with a WS row.

Change to MC, larger needles, and St st.

Next row: (RS) Knit and *at the same time* dec 14 (16, 16, 18, 18, 20) sts evenly spaced—97 (107, 119, 129, 141, 151) sts rem.

Work 3 rows even, ending with a WS row.

Change to CC and smaller needles.

Next row: (RS) Knit and *at the same time* inc 14 (16, 16, 18, 18, 20) sts evenly spaced—111 (123, 135, 147, 159, 171) sts.

Work 3 rows even, ending with a WS row.

Change to MC and larger needles.

Next row: (RS) Knit and *at the same time* dec 14 (16, 16, 18, 18, 20) sts evenly spaced—97 (107, 119, 129, 141, 151) sts rem.

Next row: (WS) P19 (21, 23, 25, 28, 30), place marker (pm), p59 (65, 73, 79, 85, 91), pm, p19 (21, 23, 25, 28, 30)—piece measures about 3½" (9 cm) from CO.

Shape Waist

Dec row: (RS) Knit to m, slip marker (sl m), ssk, knit to 2 sts before next m, k2tog, sl m, knit to end—2 sts dec'd from center section between m.

Cont in St st, rep the dec row every 4th row 5 (3, 2, 3, 2, 3) more times, then every other row 0 (4, 6, 4, 6, 4) times—85 (91, 101, 113, 123, 135) sts rem.

Work even until piece measures 9" (23 cm) from CO, ending with a WS row.

Inc row: (RS) Knit to m, sl m, M1 (see Glossary), knit to next m, M1, sl m, knit to end—2 sts inc'd in center section between markers.

Cont in St st, rep the inc row every 4th row 5 (3, 2, 3, 2, 3) more times, then every other row 0 (4, 6, 4, 6, 4) times, working new sts in St st—97 (107, 119, 129, 141, 151) sts.

Removing m on next row, work even in St st until piece measures 14½" (37 cm) from CO for all sizes, ending with a WS row.

Shape Armholes

BO 5 (5, 5, 8, 8, 8) sts at the beg of the next 2 rows, then BO 3 (3, 3, 5, 5, 5) sts at the beg of the foll 2 (4, 6, 2, 2, 2) rows—81 (85, 91, 103, 115, 125) sts rem.

BO 2 (2, 2, 3, 3, 3) sts at the beg of the next 2 (4, 4, 2, 4, 6) rows, then BO 1 (1, 1, 2, 2, 2) st(s) at the beg of the foll 6 (2, 2, 2, 2, 4) rows—71 (75, 81, 93, 99, 99) sts rem.

BO 0 (0, 0, 1, 1, 1) st at the beg of the next 0 (0, 0, 6, 6, 2) rows—71 (75, 81, 87, 93, 97) sts rem.

Work even until armholes measure 7 (7½, 8, 8½, 9, 9½)" (18 [19, 20.5, 21.5, 23, 24] cm), ending with a WS row.

Shape Neck and Shoulders

BO 3 (3, 4, 5, 5, 6) sts at the beg of the next 2 rows—65 (69, 73, 77, 83, 85) sts rem.

Next row: (RS) BO 3 (4, 4, 5, 5, 6) sts, knit until there are 18 (19, 21, 22, 24, 24) sts on right needle after BO, join new yarn and BO 23 (23, 23, 23, 25, 25) center sts, knit to end—18 (19, 21, 22, 24, 24) sts rem for right shoulder, and 21 (23, 25, 27, 29, 30) sts rem for left shoulder.

Place right shoulder sts onto holder.

Left Shoulder

Cont on sts of left shoulder only as foll.

Next row: (WS) BO 3 (4, 4, 5, 5, 6) sts, purl to end—18 (19, 21, 22, 24, 24) sts rem.

Next row: (RS) BO 6 sts at neck edge, knit to end—12 (13, 15, 16, 18, 18) sts rem.

Next row: BO 3 (4, 4, 5, 6, 6) sts, purl to end—9 (9, 11, 11, 12, 12) sts rem.

Next row: BO 5 (5, 6, 6, 6, 6) sts at neck edge, knit to end—4 (4, 5, 5, 6, 6) sts rem.

BO all sts.

Right Shoulder

Return 18 (19, 21, 22, 24, 24) held right shoulder sts to larger needle.

Next row: (WS) BO 6 sts at neck edge, purl to end—12 (13, 15, 16, 18, 18) sts rem.

Next row: BO 3 (4, 4, 5, 6, 6) sts, knit to end—9 (9, 11, 11, 12, 12) sts rem.

Next row: BO 5 (5, 6, 6, 6, 6) sts at neck edge, purl to end—4 (4, 5, 5, 6, 6) sts rem.

BO all sts.

∙∙

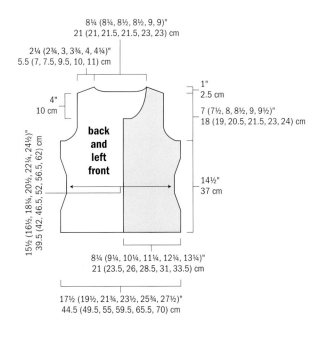

8¼ (8¼, 8½, 8½, 9, 9)"
21 (21, 21.5, 21.5, 23, 23) cm

2¼ (2¾, 3, 3¾, 4, 4¼)"
5.5 (7, 7.5, 9.5, 10, 11) cm

4"
10 cm

1"
2.5 cm

7 (7½, 8, 8½, 9, 9½)"
18 (19, 20.5, 21.5, 23, 24) cm

back and left front

15½ (16½, 18¼, 20½, 22¼, 24½)"
39.5 (42, 46.5, 52, 56.5, 62) cm

14½"
37 cm

8¼ (9¼, 10¼, 11¼, 12¼, 13¼)"
21 (23.5, 26, 28.5, 31, 33.5) cm

17½ (19½, 21¾, 23½, 25¾, 27½)"
44.5 (49.5, 55, 59.5, 65.5, 70) cm

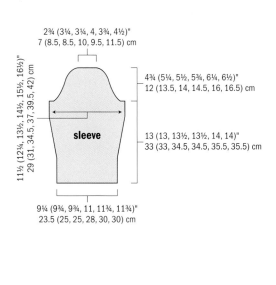

2¾ (3¼, 3¼, 4, 3¾, 4½)"
7 (8.5, 8.5, 10, 9.5, 11.5) cm

4¾ (5¼, 5½, 5¾, 6¼, 6½)"
12 (13.5, 14, 14.5, 16, 16.5) cm

11½ (12¾, 13½, 14½, 15½, 16½)"
29 (31, 34.5, 37, 39.5, 42) cm

sleeve

13 (13, 13½, 13½, 14, 14)"
33 (33, 34.5, 34.5, 35.5, 35.5) cm

9¼ (9¾, 9¾, 11, 11¾, 11¾)"
23.5 (25, 25, 28, 30, 30) cm

Left Front

With CC, smaller needles, and using the I-cord method, CO 60 (67, 74, 82, 89, 96) sts.

Next row: (WS) Purl and *at the same time* dec 9 (10, 11, 13, 14, 15) sts evenly spaced—51 (57, 63, 69, 75, 81) sts rem.

Work Rows 1–12 of Bukhara Chart A (B, A, B, A, B) 2 times, ending with a WS row.

Change to MC, larger needles, and St st.

Next row: (RS) Knit and *at the same time* dec 6 (6, 7, 7, 8, 8) sts evenly spaced—45 (51, 56, 62, 67, 73) sts rem.

Work 3 rows even, ending with a WS row.

Change to CC and smaller needles.

Next row: (RS) Knit and *at the same time* inc 6 (6, 7, 7, 8, 8) sts evenly spaced—51 (57, 63, 69, 75, 81) sts.

Work 3 rows even, ending with a WS row.

Change to MC and larger needles.

Next row: (RS) Knit and *at the same time* dec 6 (6, 7, 7, 8, 8) sts evenly spaced—45 (51, 56, 62, 67, 73) sts rem.

Next row: (WS) P26 (30, 33, 37, 39, 43), pm, p19 (21, 23, 25, 28, 30)—piece measures about 3½" (9 cm) from CO.

Shape Waist

Dec row: (RS) Knit to m, sl m, ssk, knit to end—1 st dec'd.

Cont in St st, rep the dec row every 4th row 5 (3, 2, 3, 2, 3) more times, then every other row 0 (4, 6, 4, 6, 4) times—39 (43, 47, 54, 58, 65) sts rem.

Work even until piece measures 9" (23 cm) from CO, ending with a WS row.

Inc row: (RS) Knit to m, sl m, M1, knit to end—1 st inc'd.

☐ knit on RS; purl on WS

• purl on RS; knit on WS

◇ place bead (see Stitch Guide)

☐ pattern repeat

BUKHARA CHART A

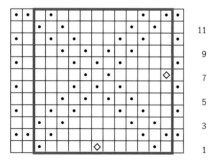

BUKHARA CHART B

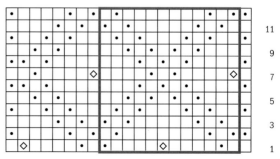

Cont in St st, rep the inc row every 4th row 5 (3, 2, 3, 2, 3) more times, then every other row 0 (4, 6, 4, 6, 4) times, working new sts in St st—45 (51, 56, 62, 67, 73) sts.

Removing m on next row, work even in St st until piece measures 14½" (37 cm) from CO for all sizes, ending with a WS row.

Shape Armhole

BO 5 (5, 5, 8, 8, 8) sts at the beg of the next RS row, then BO 3 (3, 3, 5, 5, 5) sts at the beg of the foll 1 (2, 3, 1, 1, 1) RS row(s)—37 (40, 42, 49, 54, 60) sts rem.

BO 2 (2, 2, 3, 3, 3) sts at the beg of the next 1 (2, 2, 1, 2, 3) RS row(s), then BO 1 (1, 1, 2, 2, 2) st(s) at the beg of the foll 3 (1, 1, 1, 1, 2) RS row(s)—32 (35, 37, 44, 46, 47) sts rem.

BO 0 (0, 0, 1, 1, 1) st at the beg of the next 0 (0, 0, 3, 3, 1) RS row(s)—32 (35, 37, 41, 43, 46) sts rem.

Work even until armhole measures 3 (3½, 4, 4½, 5, 5½)" (7.5 [9, 10, 11.5, 12.5, 14] cm), ending with a RS row.

Shape Neck

At neck edge (beg of WS rows), BO 6 (7, 7, 7, 7, 8) sts once, then BO 4 (4, 4, 5, 5, 5) sts once, then BO 3 sts once, then BO 2 sts once, then BO 1 st 4 times—13 (15, 17, 20, 22, 24) sts rem.

Work even until armhole measures 7 (7½, 8, 8½, 9, 9½)" (18 [19, 20.5, 21.5, 23, 24] cm), ending with a WS row.

Shape Shoulder

At armhole edge (beg of RS rows), BO 3 (3, 4, 5, 5, 6) sts once, then BO 3 (4, 4, 5, 5, 6) sts once, then BO 3 (4, 5, 5, 6, 6) sts once, then BO 4 (4, 5, 5, 6, 6) sts once—no sts rem.

Right Front

With CC, smaller needles, and using the I-cord method, CO 60 (67, 74, 82, 89, 96) sts.

Next row: (WS) Purl and *at the same time* dec 9 (10, 11, 13, 14, 15) sts evenly spaced—51 (57, 63, 69, 75, 81) sts rem.

Work Rows 1–12 of Bukhara Chart A (B, A, B, A, B) 2 times, ending with a WS row.

Change to MC, larger needles, and St st.

Next row: (RS) Knit and *at the same time* dec 6 (6, 7, 7, 8, 8) sts evenly spaced—45 (51, 56, 62, 67, 73) sts rem.

Work 3 rows even, ending with a WS row.

Change to CC and smaller needles.

Next row: (RS) Knit and *at the same time* inc 6 (6, 7, 7, 8, 8) sts evenly spaced—51 (57, 63, 69, 75, 81) sts.

Work 3 rows even, ending with a WS row.

Change to MC and larger needles.

Next row: (RS) Knit and *at the same time* dec 6 (6, 7, 7, 8, 8) sts evenly spaced—45 (51, 56, 62, 67, 73) sts rem.

Next row: (WS) P19 (21, 23, 25, 28, 30), pm, p26 (30, 33, 37, 39, 43)—piece measures about 3½" (9 cm) from CO.

Shape Waist

Dec row: (RS) Knit to 2 sts before m, k2tog, sl m, knit to end—1 st dec'd.

Cont in St st, rep the dec row every 4th row 5 (3, 2, 3, 2, 3) more times, then every other row 0 (4, 6, 4, 6, 4) times—39 (43, 47, 54, 58, 65) sts rem.

Work even until piece measures 9" (23 cm) from CO, ending with a WS row.

Inc row: (RS) Knit to m, M1, sl m, knit to end—1 st inc'd.

Cont in St st, rep the inc row every 4th row 5 (3, 2, 3, 2, 3) more times, then every other row 0 (4, 6, 4, 6, 4) times, working new sts in St st—45 (51, 56, 62, 67, 73) sts.

Removing m on next row, work even in St st until piece measures 14½" (37 cm) from CO for all sizes, ending with a RS row.

Shape Armhole

BO 5 (5, 5, 8, 8, 8) sts at the beg of the next WS row, then BO 3 (3, 3, 5, 5, 5) sts at the beg of the foll 1 (2, 3, 1, 1, 1) WS row(s)—37 (40, 42, 49, 54, 60) sts rem.

BO 2 (2, 2, 3, 3, 3) sts at the beg of the next 1 (2, 2, 1, 2, 3) WS row(s), then BO 1 (1, 1, 2, 2, 2) st(s) at the beg of the foll 3 (1, 1, 1, 1, 2) WS row(s)—32 (35, 37, 44, 46, 47) sts rem.

BO 0 (0, 0, 1, 1, 1) st at the beg of the next 0 (0, 0, 3, 3, 1) WS row(s)—32 (35, 37, 41, 43, 46) sts rem.

Work even until armhole measures 3 (3½, 4, 4½, 5, 5½)" (7.5 [9, 10, 11.5, 12.5, 14] cm), ending with a WS row.

Shape Neck

At neck edge (beg of RS rows), BO 6 (7, 7, 7, 7, 8) sts once, then BO 4 (4, 4, 5, 5, 5) sts once, then BO 3 sts once, then BO 2 sts once, then BO 1 st 4 times—13 (15, 17, 20, 22, 24) sts rem.

Work even until armhole measures 7 (7½, 8, 8½, 9, 9½)" (18 [19, 20.5, 21.5, 23, 24] cm), ending with a RS row.

Shape Shoulder

At armhole edge (beg of WS rows), BO 3 (3, 4, 5, 5, 6) sts once, then BO 3 (4, 4, 5, 5, 6) sts once, then BO 3 (4, 4, 5, 6, 6) sts once, then BO 4 (4, 5, 5, 6, 6) sts once—no sts rem.

Sleeves

With CC, smaller needles, and using the I-cord method, CO 67 (70, 70, 78, 87, 87) sts.

Next row: (WS) Purl and *at the same time* dec 10 (7, 7, 9, 12, 12) sts evenly spaced—57 (63, 63, 69, 75, 75) sts rem.

Work Rows 1–12 of Bukhara Chart B (A, A, B, A, A) 2 times, ending with a WS row.

Change to MC, larger needles, and St st.

Next row: (RS) Knit and *at the same time* dec 6 (9, 9, 9, 10, 10) sts evenly spaced—51 (54, 54, 60, 65, 65) sts rem.

Work 3 rows even, ending with a WS row.

Change to CC and smaller needles.

Next row: (RS) Knit and *at the same time* inc 6 (9, 9, 9, 10, 10) sts evenly spaced—57 (63, 63, 69, 75, 75) sts.

Work 3 rows even, ending with a WS row.

Change to MC and larger needles.

Next row: (RS) Knit and *at the same time* dec 6 (9, 7, 9, 10, 8) sts evenly spaced—51 (54, 56, 60, 65, 67) sts rem.

Work even in St st until piece measures 4" (10 cm) from CO, ending with a WS row.

Inc row: (RS) K1, M1, knit to last st, M1, k1—2 sts inc'd.

Rep inc row every 4th row 0 (0, 0, 0, 0, 4) times, then every 6th row 0 (0, 7, 9, 9, 7) times, then every 8th row 3 (6, 1, 0, 0, 0) time(s), then every 10th row 2 (0, 0, 0, 0, 0) times—63 (68, 74, 80, 85, 91) sts.

Work even until piece measures 13 (13, 13½, 13½,

14, 14)" (33 [33, 34.5, 34.5, 35.5, 35.5] cm) from CO, ending with a WS row.

Shape Cap

BO 5 (5, 5, 8, 8, 8) sts at the beg of the next 2 rows—53 (58, 64, 64, 69, 75) sts rem.

*BO 2 sts at the beg of the next 2 rows, then BO 1 st at the beg of the foll 2 rows, then work 2 rows even; rep from * 2 (2, 2, 2, 0, 0) more times—35 (40, 46, 46, 63, 69) sts rem.

*BO 1 st at beg of next 2 rows, then work 2 rows even; rep from * 1 (2, 2, 3, 6, 7) more time(s)—31 (34, 40, 38, 49, 53) sts rem.

BO 1 st at the beg of the next 4 rows, then BO 3 (3, 3, 3, 4, 4) sts at the beg of the next 4 (4, 6, 4, 6, 6) rows—15 (18, 18, 22, 21, 25) sts rem.

BO all sts.

Finishing

Block to measurements. With MC threaded on a tapestry needle, sew side seams. Sew shoulder seams. Sew sleeve seams. Sew sleeve caps into armholes, matching center of cap BO with shoulder seam and matching sleeve seam with side seam at underarm.

Neckband

With MC, larger needle, and RS facing, pick up and knit 128 (136, 148, 156, 168, 176) sts evenly spaced along neck edge.

Next row: (WS) *K1, p1; rep from *.

Cont in k1, p1 rib (knit the knits, and purl the purls) until piece measures 1" (2.5 cm) from pick-up row.

BO all sts in patt.

Buttonband

With MC, larger needle, and RS facing, pick up and knit 104 (106, 110, 112, 116, 118) sts evenly spaced along left front edge. Work in k1, p1 rib as for neckband until piece measures 1" (2.5 cm) from pick-up row.

BO all sts in patt. Mark band for 7 buttons, placing the top button ½" (1.3 cm) below neck edge, lowest

button ½" (1.3 cm) up from lower edge, and the rem 5 evenly spaced between.

Buttonhole Band

With MC, larger needle, and RS facing, pick up and knit 104 (106, 110, 112, 116, 118) sts evenly spaced along right front edge. Work in k1, p1 rib as for neckband for 2 rows.

Next row: (WS) Cont in rib, working a [yo, p2tog] buttonhole opposite each marked button position on buttonband.

Cont in rib until band measures 1" (2.5 cm) from pick-up row.

BO all sts in patt.

Weave in loose ends.

Neckline Beads

Note: *See Sewing Beads or Sequins onto Knitted Fabric on page 18.*

With matching thread and sharp-point sewing needle, sew an irregularly spaced line of beads about 1½" (3.8 cm) away from and parallel to the neckband pick-up row, with the beads ⅜" (1 cm) to 1" (2.5 cm) apart. This line marks the boundary of the beaded area. Using sewing needle and thread, fill in the area between the boundary line and the neckband with randomly chosen beads as shown, placing each bead at least ¼" (6 mm) away from its closest neighbors. As a general guideline, the cardigan shown used about 90 beads on each front, and about 150 beads on the back, but your numbers may be different depending on your chosen placement and garment size.

Sew buttons to buttonband opposite buttonholes.

Aswan

dress with tunic option

Finished Size
About 35 (38¾, 43, 46¾, 51, 54¾)" (89 [98.5, 109, 118.5, 129.5, 139] cm) bust circumference, including 1" (2.5 cm) front band.

Designed to be worn with about 3" (7.5 cm) of positive ease at the bust.

Dress shown measures 35" (89 cm).

Yarn
Fingering weight (#1 Super Fine) and DK weight (#3 Light).

Shown here: Rowan Kidsilk Haze (70% super kid mohair, 30% silk; 229 yd [209 m]/25 g): #652 Mud (MC, medium golden brown), 6 (7, 8, 8, 9, 10) balls for dress length; 5 (5, 6, 7, 7, 8) balls for tunic length.

Louisa Harding Grace Silk & Wool (50% silk, 50% merino; 110 yd [101 m]/50 g): #44 Frenchie (CC, blue), 2 (2, 3, 3, 3, 3) balls for dress length; 2 balls all sizes for tunic length.

Needles
Body and sleeves: size U.S. 3 (3.25 mm).

Edging: size U.S. 6 (4 mm).

Adjust needle size if necessary to obtain the correct gauge.

Notions
Markers (m), removable markers, tapestry needle, ten ¾" (2 cm) buttons for dress length; seven ¾" (2 cm) buttons for tunic length.

Gauge
22 sts and 34 rows = 4" (10 cm) in St st on smaller needles with MC.

This standard-fitting dress is knitted in featherlight mohair with contrasting edgings. The pieces are worked separately, then seamed together. Waist shaping and a button-front closure add to the visual sleekness. Instructions are provided for a shorter tunic length for an alternative look.

The tunic-length version is not shown in the photographs.

The schematic shows the pieces without edgings for blocking purposes. The edgings at the lower edge and cuffs will add about 1" (2.5 cm) to the lengths of the body and sleeves.

Refer to Chapter 1 for general knitting foundations.

Back

Dress length

With MC and smaller needles, CO 124 (134, 146, 156, 168, 178) sts. Work in St st (knit RS rows; purl WS rows) until piece measures 1" (2.5 cm) from CO, ending with a WS row.

Dec row: (RS) K1, ssk, knit to last 3 sts, k2tog, k1—2 sts dec'd.

Rep dec row every 8th row 4 more times, then every 6th row 6 times—102 (112, 124, 134, 146, 156) sts rem; piece measures 9" (23 cm) from CO. Work even until piece measures 10¾" (27.5 cm) from CO, ending with a WS row.

Tunic length

With MC and smaller needles, CO 102 (112, 124, 134, 146, 156) sts. Work in St st until piece measures 1" (2.5 cm) from CO, ending with a WS row.

Both lengths

Dec row: (RS) K1, ssk, knit to last 3 sts, k2tog, k1—2 sts dec'd.

Rep dec row every 8th row 5 more times, then every 6th row 5 times—80 (90, 102, 112, 124, 134) sts rem; piece measures 19" (48.5 cm) from CO for dress length or 9¼" (23.5 cm) from CO for tunic length.

Work even until piece measures 20¾" (52.5 cm) from CO for dress length or 11" (28 cm) from CO for tunic length, ending with a WS row.

Inc row: (RS) K1, M1 (see Glossary), knit to last st, M1, k1—2 sts inc'd.

Rep inc row every 8th row 4 more times, then every 6th row 3 times, working new sts in St st—96 (106, 118, 128, 140, 150) sts.

Work even until piece measures 28½" (72.5 cm) from CO for dress length or 18¾" (47.5 cm) from CO for tunic length, ending with a WS row.

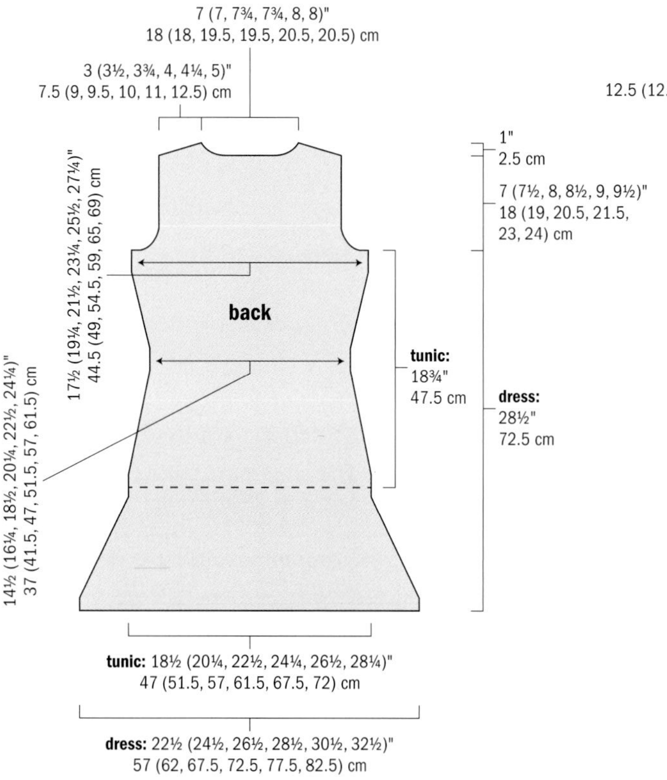

7 (7, 7¾, 7¾, 8, 8)"
18 (18, 19.5, 19.5, 20.5, 20.5) cm
3 (3½, 3¾, 4, 4¼, 5)"
7.5 (9, 9.5, 10, 11, 12.5) cm
1"
2.5 cm
7 (7½, 8, 8½, 9, 9½)"
18 (19, 20.5, 21.5, 23, 24) cm
17½ (19¼, 21½, 23¼, 25½, 27¼)"
44.5 (49, 54.5, 59, 65, 69) cm
back
14½ (16¼, 18½, 20¼, 22½, 24¼)"
37 (41.5, 47, 51.5, 57, 61.5) cm
tunic:
18¾"
47.5 cm
dress:
28½"
72.5 cm
tunic: 18½ (20¼, 22½, 24¼, 26½, 28¼)"
47 (51.5, 57, 61.5, 67.5, 72) cm
dress: 22½ (24½, 26½, 28½, 30½, 32½)"
57 (62, 67.5, 72.5, 77.5, 82.5) cm

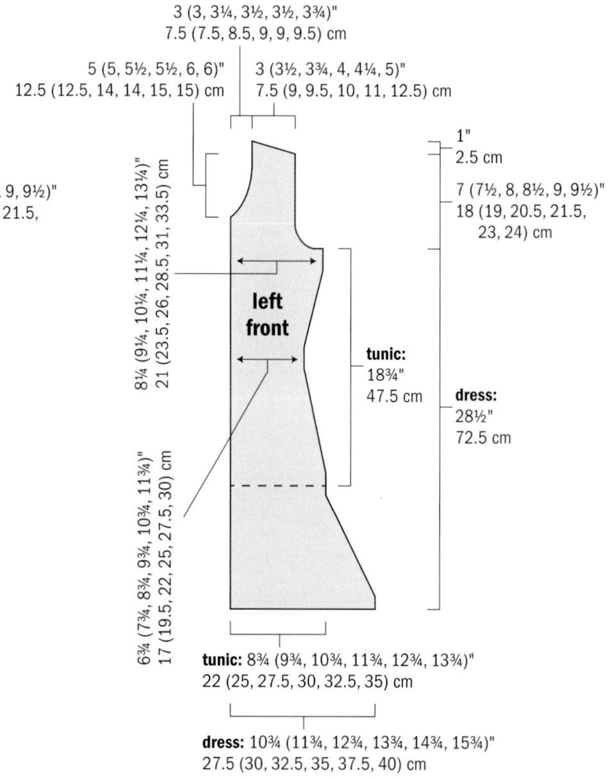

3 (3, 3¼, 3½, 3½, 3¾)"
7.5 (7.5, 8.5, 9, 9, 9.5) cm
5 (5, 5½, 5½, 6, 6)"
12.5 (12.5, 14, 14, 15, 15) cm
3 (3½, 3¾, 4, 4¼, 5)"
7.5 (9, 9.5, 10, 11, 12.5) cm
1"
2.5 cm
7 (7½, 8, 8½, 9, 9½)"
18 (19, 20.5, 21.5, 23, 24) cm
8¼ (9¼, 10¼, 11¼, 12¾, 13¾)"
21 (23.5, 26, 28.5, 31, 33.5) cm
left front
6¾ (7¾, 8¾, 9¾, 10¾, 11¾)"
17 (19.5, 22, 25, 27.5, 30) cm
tunic:
18¾"
47.5 cm
dress:
28½"
72.5 cm
tunic: 8¾ (9¾, 10¾, 11¾, 12¾, 13¾)"
22 (25, 27.5, 30, 32.5, 35) cm
dress: 10¾ (11¾, 12¾, 13¾, 14¾, 15¾)"
27.5 (30, 32.5, 35, 37.5, 40) cm

Shape Armholes

BO 6 (6, 6, 9, 9, 9) sts at the beg of the next 2 rows, then BO 3 (3, 3, 3, 3, 4) sts at the beg of the foll 2 (2, 4, 4, 6, 4) rows—78 (88, 94, 98, 104, 116) sts rem.

BO 2 (2, 2, 2, 2, 3) sts at the beg of the next 2 (4, 4, 4, 4, 2) rows, then BO 1 (1, 1, 1, 1, 2) st(s) at the beg of the foll 4 rows—70 (76, 82, 86, 92, 102) sts rem.

BO 0 (0, 0, 0, 0, 1) st(s) at the beg of the next 0 (0, 0, 0, 0, 4) rows—70 (76, 82, 86, 92, 98) sts rem.

Work even until armholes measure 7 (7½, 8, 8½, 9, 9½)" (18 [19, 20.5, 21.5, 23, 24] cm), ending with a WS row.

Shape Neck and Shoulders

Note: *Neck and shoulders are shaped at the same time; read all the way through the following section before proceeding.*

With RS facing, k25 (28, 30, 32, 35, 38), join new yarn and BO 20 (20, 22, 22, 22, 22) sts, knit to end—25 (28, 30, 32, 35, 38) sts rem each side.

Working each side separately, at each armhole edge BO 4 (5, 5, 6, 6, 7) sts 2 times, then 4 (5, 5, 5, 6, 7) sts once, then 4 (4, 5, 5, 6, 6) sts once. *At the same time,* at each neck edge, BO 5 (5, 5, 5, 6, 6) sts once, then 4 (4, 5, 5, 5, 5) sts once—no sts rem.

. . . .

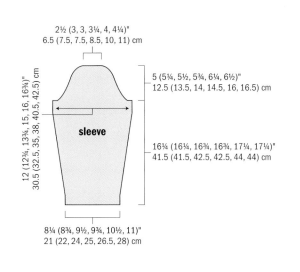

2½ (3, 3, 3¼, 4, 4¼)"
6.5 (7.5, 7.5, 8.5, 10, 11) cm

5 (5¼, 5½, 5¾, 6¼, 6½)"
12.5 (13.5, 14, 14.5, 16, 16.5) cm

12 (12¾, 13¾, 15, 16, 16¾)"
30.5 (32.5, 35, 38, 40.5, 42.5) cm

sleeve

16¼ (16¼, 16¾, 16¾, 17¼, 17¼)"
41.5 (41.5, 42.5, 42.5, 44, 44) cm

8¼ (8¾, 9½, 9¾, 10½, 11)"
21 (22, 24, 25, 26.5, 28) cm

Left Front

Dress length

With MC and smaller needles, CO 59 (65, 70, 76, 81, 87) sts. Work in St st until piece measures 1" (2.5 cm) from CO, ending with a WS row.

Dec row: (RS) K1, ssk, knit to end—1 st dec'd.

Rep dec row every 8th row 4 more times, then every 6th row 6 times—48 (54, 59, 65, 70, 76) sts rem; piece measures 9" (23 cm) from CO. Work even until piece measures 10¾" (27.5 cm) from CO, ending with a WS row.

Tunic length

With MC and smaller needles, CO 48 (54, 59, 65, 70, 76) sts. Work in St st until piece measures 1" (2.5 cm) from CO, ending with a WS row.

Both lengths

Dec row: (RS) K1, ssk, knit to end—1 st dec'd.

Rep dec row every 8th row 5 more times, then every 6th row 5 times—37 (43, 48, 54, 59, 65) sts rem;

piece measures 19" (48.5 cm) from CO for dress length or 9¼" (23.5 cm) from CO for tunic length.

Work even until piece measures 20¾" (52.5 cm) from CO for dress length or 11" (28 cm) from CO for tunic length, ending with a WS row.

Inc row: (RS) K1, M1, knit to end—1 st inc'd.

Rep inc row every 8th row 4 more times, then every 6th row 3 times, working new sts in St st—45 (51, 56, 62, 67, 73) sts.

Work even until piece measures 28½" (72.5 cm) from CO for dress length or 18¾" (47.5 cm) from CO for tunic length, ending with a WS row.

Shape Armhole

At armhole edge (beg of RS rows), BO 6 (6, 6, 9, 9, 9) sts once, then BO 3 (3, 3, 3, 3, 4) sts 1 (1, 2, 2, 3, 2) time(s)—36 (42, 44, 47, 49, 56) sts rem.

BO 2 (2, 2, 2, 2, 3) sts at the beg of the next 1 (2, 2, 2, 2, 1) RS row(s), then BO 1 (1, 1, 1, 1, 2) st(s) at the beg of the foll 2 RS rows—32 (36, 38, 41, 43, 49) sts rem.

BO 0 (0, 0, 0, 0, 1) st(s) at the beg of the next 0 (0, 0, 0, 0, 2) RS rows—32 (36, 38, 41, 43, 47) sts rem.

Work even until armhole measures 2 (2½, 2½, 3, 3, 3½)" (5 [6.5, 6.5, 7.5, 7.5, 9] cm), ending with a RS row.

Shape Neck

At neck edge (beg of WS rows), dec 1 st 16 (17, 18, 19, 19, 20) times—16 (19, 20, 22, 24, 27) sts rem.

Work even until armhole measures 7 (7½, 8, 8½, 9, 9½)" (18 [19, 20.5, 21.5, 23, 24] cm), ending with a WS row.

Shape Shoulder

At armhole edge (beg of RS rows), BO 4 (5, 5, 6, 6, 7) sts 2 times, then BO 4 (5, 5, 5, 6, 7) sts once, then BO 4 (4, 5, 5, 6, 6) sts once—no sts rem.

Right Front

Dress length

With MC and smaller needles, CO 59 (65, 70, 76, 81, 87) sts. Work in St st until piece measures 1" (2.5 cm) from CO, ending with a WS row.

Dec row: (RS) Knit to last 3 sts, k2tog, k1—1 st dec'd.

Rep dec row every 8th row 4 more times, then every 6th row 6 times—48 (54, 59, 65, 70, 76) sts rem; piece measures 9" (23 cm) from CO. Work even until piece measures 10¾" (27.5 cm) from CO, ending with a WS row.

Tunic length

With MC and smaller needles, CO 48 (54, 59, 65, 70, 76) sts. Work in St st until piece measures 1" (2.5 cm) from CO, ending with a WS row.

Both lengths

Dec row: (RS) Knit to last 3 sts, k2tog, k1—1 st dec'd.

Rep dec row every 8th row 5 more times, then every 6th row 5 times—37 (43, 48, 54, 59, 65) sts rem; piece measures 19" (48.5 cm) from CO for dress length or 9¼" (23.5 cm) from CO for tunic length.

Work even until piece measures 20¾" (52.5 cm) from CO for dress length or 11" (28 cm) from CO for tunic length, ending with a WS row.

Inc row: (RS) Knit to last st, M1, k1—1 st inc'd.

Rep inc row every 8th row 4 more times, then every 6th row 3 times, working new sts in St st—45 (51, 56, 62, 67, 73) sts.

Work even until piece measures 28½" (72.5 cm) from CO for dress length or 18¾" (47.5 cm) from CO for tunic length, ending with a RS row.

Shape Armhole

At armhole edge (beg of WS rows), BO 6 (6, 6, 9, 9, 9) sts once, then BO 3 (3, 3, 3, 3, 4) sts 1 (1, 2, 2, 3, 2) time(s)—36 (42, 44, 47, 49, 56) sts rem.

BO 2 (2, 2, 2, 2, 3) sts at the beg of the next 1 (2, 2, 2, 2, 1) WS row(s), then BO 1 (1, 1, 1, 1, 2) st(s) at the beg of the foll 2 WS rows—32 (36, 38, 41, 43, 49) sts rem.

BO 0 (0, 0, 0, 0, 1) st(s) at the beg of the next 0 (0, 0, 0, 0, 2) WS rows—32 (36, 38, 41, 43, 47) sts rem.

Work even until armhole measures 2 (2½, 2½, 3, 3, 3½)" (5 [6.5, 6.5, 7.5, 7.5, 9] cm), ending with a WS row.

Shape Neck

At neck edge (beg of RS rows), dec 1 st 16 (17, 18, 19, 19, 20) times—16 (19, 20, 22, 24, 27) sts rem.

Work even until armhole measures 7 (7½, 8, 8½, 9, 9½)" (18 [19, 20.5, 21.5, 23, 24] cm), ending with a RS row.

Shape Shoulder

At armhole edge (beg of WS rows) BO 4 (5, 5, 6, 6, 7) sts 2 times, then BO 4 (5, 5, 5, 6, 7) sts once, then BO 4 (4, 5, 5, 6, 6) sts once—no sts rem.

Sleeves

With MC and smaller needles, CO 46 (48, 52, 54, 58, 60) sts. Work in St st until piece measures 1½" (3.8 cm) from CO, ending with a WS row.

Inc row: (RS) K1, M1, knit to last st, M1, k1—2 sts inc'd.

Rep inc row every 10 (10, 10, 8, 8, 8)th row 3 (5, 9, 6, 9, 14) times, then every 12 (12, 12, 10, 10, 10)th row 6 (5, 2, 7, 5, 1) time(s), working new sts in St st—66 (70, 76, 82, 88, 92) sts.

Work even until piece measures 16¼ (16¼, 16¾, 16¾, 17¼, 17¼)" (41.5 [41.5, 42.5, 42.5, 44, 44] cm) from CO, or 1" (2.5 cm) less than desired length to underarm (see Notes), ending with a WS row.

Shape Cap

BO 6 (6, 9, 9, 9, 9) sts at the beg of the next 2 rows—54 (58, 64, 64, 70, 74) sts rem.

Work 2 rows even, ending with a WS row.

Dec 1 st at each edge every RS row 11 (12, 16, 13, 17, 18) times, then work 1 WS row even after last dec row—32 (34, 32, 38, 36, 38) sts rem.

Dec 1 st at each edge every 4th row 3 (3, 2, 4, 3, 3) times—26 (28, 28, 30, 30, 32) sts rem.

BO 3 (3, 3, 3, 2, 2) sts at the beg of the next 4 rows—14 (16, 16, 18, 22, 24) sts rem.

BO all sts.

Finishing

Block to measurements (see Notes).

With yarn threaded on a tapestry needle, sew side seams. Sew shoulder seams.

Lower Body Edging

With CC and larger needles, pick up and knit 236 (258, 280, 302, 324, 346) sts evenly spaced around lower edge of dress body, or 198 (220, 242, 262, 286, 308) sts evenly spaced around lower edge of tunic body. Work in garter st (knit every row) for 1" (2.5 cm), ending with a WS row.

BO all sts.

Front Bands

Use removable markers to mark placement of 10 buttonholes on right dress front, or 7 buttonholes on right tunic front, with the top button ¾" (2 cm) below start of neck shaping, the lowest ¾" (2 cm) up from lower body CO edge, and the others evenly spaced in between.

With CC, larger needles, RS facing, and beg at lower right front corner, pick up and knit 138 (142, 142, 144, 144, 146) sts evenly spaced along right dress front or 92 (94, 94, 96, 96, 98) sts evenly spaced along right tunic front, pm at base of neck shaping, 38 (42, 44, 46, 50, 52) sts along right front neck, 38 (38, 42, 42, 44, 44) sts across back neck, 38 (42, 44, 46, 50, 52) sts along left front neck, pm at base of neck shaping, and 138 (142, 142, 144, 144, 146) sts along left dress front or 92 (94, 94, 96, 96, 98) sts along left tunic front—390 (406, 414, 422, 432, 440) dress sts or 298 (310, 318, 326, 336, 344) tunic sts.

Knit 1 WS row.

Inc row: (RS) Knit to m, M1, k1, M1, knit to 1 st before next m, M1, k1, M1, knit to end—4 sts inc'd.

Rep the last 2 rows once more, ending with a RS row—398 (414, 422, 430, 440, 448) dress sts or 306 (318, 326, 334, 344, 352) tunic sts.

Buttonhole row: (WS) Knit, working a [yo, k2tog] buttonhole at each marked position on right front.

Next row: (RS) Knit to m, M1, k1, M1, knit to 1 st before next m, M1, k1, M1, knit to end—4 sts inc'd.

Knit 1 WS row.

Rep the last 2 rows once more—406 (422, 430, 438, 448, 456) dress sts or 314 (326, 334, 342, 352, 360) tunic sts.

BO all sts.

Sleeve Edging

With CC and larger needles, pick up and knit 46 (48, 52, 54, 58, 60) sts evenly spaced along CO edge of sleeve. Work in garter st for 1" (2.5 cm), ending with a WS row. BO all sts.

Sew sleeve seams. Sew sleeve caps into armholes, matching center of cap BO with shoulder seam and matching sleeve seam with side seam at underarm.

Weave in loose ends. Sew buttons to left front band opposite buttonholes.

Madingley
shawl-neck cardigan

Finished Size
About 35 (38¾, 43¼, 46½, 50½, 54¼)" (89 [98.5, 110, 118, 128.5, 138] cm) bust circumference, including 2" (5 cm) front band.

Designed to be worn with about 3" (7.5 cm) of positive ease.

Cardigan shown measures 35" (89 cm).

Yarn
Worsted weight (#4 Medium).

Shown here: Berroco Blackstone Tweed (65% wool, 25% mohair, 10% angora; 130 yd [119 m]/50 g): #2601 Clover Honey (MC; tan), 7 (8, 9, 10, 10, 11) balls; #2656 Narragansett (CC; navy), 3 (3, 4, 4, 5, 5) balls.

Needles
Body, sleeves, front bands, and collar: size U.S. 6 (4 mm): 32" (80 cm) circular (cir).

Edgings: size U.S. 7 (4.5 mm).

Adjust needle size if necessary to obtain the correct gauge.

Notions
Markers (m); removable markers; six 1⅛" (28 mm) buttons; tapestry needle.

Gauge
17 sts and 27 rows = 4" (10 cm) in seed stitch on smaller needle.

19 (19, 24, 24, 29, 29) lower body edging sts measure about 2½ (2½, 3¼, 3¼, 4, 4)" (6.5 [6.5, 8.5, 8.5, 10, 10] cm) wide on larger needle.

This casual cardigan features contrasting edgings and a deep V-neck. The edgings are worked sideways in a ribbed pattern, then stitches are picked up for the body and sleeves, which are worked in seed stitch. The front bands and shawl collar are worked in a single piece in a k3, p2 rib pattern.

Refer to Chapter 1 for general knitting foundations.

Seed Stitch (even number of sts)

Row 1: (RS) *K1, p1; rep from *.

Row 2: (WS) *P1, k1; rep from *.

Rep Rows 1 and 2 for patt.

Seed Stitch (odd number of sts)

All rows: (RS and WS) K1, *p1, k1; rep from *.

Rep this row for patt.

Back

With CC and larger needle, CO 19 (19, 24, 24, 29, 29) sts. Do not join.

Row 1: (RS) *K3, p2; rep from * to last 4 sts, k4.

Row 2: (WS) K1 (garter selvedge st), p3, *k2, p3; rep from *.

Rep the last 2 rows until piece measures 17½ (19¼, 21¾, 23½, 25½, 27¼)" (44.5 [49, 55, 59.5, 65, 69] cm) from CO, ending with a WS row. BO all sts.

With MC, smaller needle, and RS facing, pick up and knit 74 (82, 92, 100, 108, 116) sts evenly spaced along garter selvedge (end of RS rows; beg of WS rows) of edging piece. Do not join.

Work even in seed st (see Stitch Guide) until piece measures 15 (15, 14¼, 14¼, 13½, 13½)" (38 [38, 36, 36, 34.5, 34.5] cm) from pick-up row and about 17½" (44.5 cm) from edging lower selvedge for all sizes, ending with a WS row.

Shape Armholes

BO 4 (4, 4, 6, 6, 6) sts at the beg of the next 2 rows, then BO 2 (3, 3, 3, 4, 4) sts at the beg of the foll 2 rows—62 (68, 78, 82, 88, 96) sts rem.

BO 0 (2, 2, 2, 3, 3) sts at the beg of the next 0 (2, 4, 4, 2, 4) rows, then BO 0 (0, 0, 0, 2, 2) sts at the beg of the foll 0 (0, 0, 0, 4, 6) rows—62 (64, 70, 74, 74, 72) sts rem.

Dec 1 st at each armhole edge every RS row 4 (3, 4, 4, 3, 2) times—54 (58, 62, 66, 68, 68) sts rem.

Work even until armholes measure 7 (7½, 8, 8½, 9, 9½)" (18 [19, 20.5, 21.5, 23, 24] cm), ending with a WS row.

Shape Neck and Shoulders

Note: *Neck shaping is worked at the same time as shoulder shaping; read all the way through the foll section before proceeding.*

Next row: (RS) Keeping in patt, work 18 (20, 21, 23, 23, 23) sts, join new ball of yarn and BO 18 (18, 20, 20, 22, 22) center sts for back neck, work in patt to end—18 (20, 21, 23, 23, 23) sts rem each side.

Working each side separately, at each armhole edge BO 3 (3, 3, 4, 4, 4) sts once, then BO 3 (3, 3, 4, 3, 3) sts once, then BO 2 (3, 3, 3, 3, 3) sts 2 times, and *at the same time* at each neck edge BO 4 (4, 5, 5, 5, 5) sts once, then BO 4 (4, 4, 4, 5, 5) sts once—no sts rem.

Left Front

With CC and larger needle, CO 19 (19, 24, 24, 29, 29) sts. Do not join.

Rep edging Rows 1 and 2 as for back until piece measures 7¾ (8¾, 9¾, 10½, 11½, 12½)" (19.5 [22, 25, 26.5, 29, 31.5] cm) from CO, ending with a WS row.

BO all sts.

With MC, smaller needle, and RS facing, pick up and knit 33 (37, 41, 45, 49, 53) sts evenly spaced along garter selvedge of edging piece. Do not join.

Work even in seed st (see Stitch Guide) until piece measures 13½ (13½, 12¾, 12¾, 12, 12)" (34.5 [34.5, 32.5, 32.5, 30.5, 30.5] cm) from pick-up row and about 16" (40.5 cm) from edging lower selvedge for all sizes, ending with a RS row.

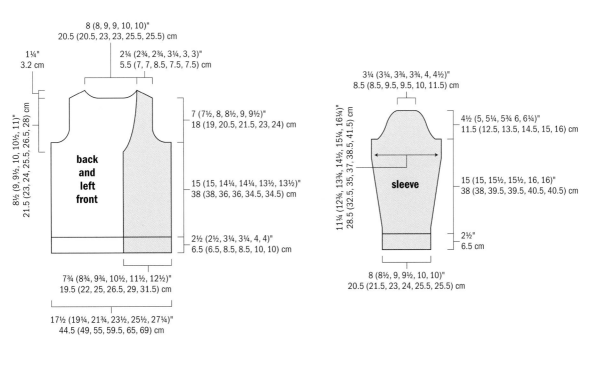

8 (8, 9, 9, 10, 10)"
20.5 (20.5, 23, 23, 25.5, 25.5) cm

1¼"
3.2 cm

2¼ (2¾, 2¾, 3¼, 3, 3)"
5.5 (7, 7, 8.5, 7.5, 7.5) cm

7 (7½, 8, 8½, 9, 9½)"
18 (19, 20.5, 21.5, 23, 24) cm

8½ (9, 9½, 10, 10½, 11)"
21.5 (23, 24, 25.5, 26.5, 28) cm

back and left front

15 (15, 14¼, 14¼, 13½, 13½)"
38 (38, 36, 36, 34.5, 34.5) cm

2½ (2½, 3¼, 3¼, 4, 4)"
6.5 (6.5, 8.5, 8.5, 10, 10) cm

7¾ (8¾, 9¾, 10½, 11½, 12½)"
19.5 (22, 25, 26.5, 29, 31.5) cm

17½ (19¼, 21¾, 23½, 25½, 27¼)"
44.5 (49, 55, 59.5, 65, 69) cm

3¼ (3¼, 3¾, 3¾, 4, 4½)"
8.5 (8.5, 9.5, 9.5, 10, 11.5) cm

4½ (5, 5¼, 5¾ 6, 6¼)"
11.5 (12.5, 13.5, 14.5, 15, 16) cm

11¼ (12¾, 13¾, 14½, 15¼, 16¼)"
28.5 (32.5, 35, 37, 38.5, 41.5) cm

sleeve

15 (15, 15½, 15½, 16, 16)"
38 (38, 39.5, 39.5, 40.5, 40.5) cm

2½"
6.5 cm

8 (8½, 9, 9½, 10, 10)"
20.5 (21.5, 23, 24, 25.5, 25.5) cm

Shape Armhole and Neck

Note: *Armhole shaping is introduced while neck shaping is in progress; read all the way through the foll section before proceeding.*

Neck dec row: (WS) K1, p2tog through back loops (tbl), work in patt to end—1 st dec'd.

Rep neck dec row every 4th row 7 (9, 10, 12, 11, 11) more times, then every other row 5 (3, 3, 1, 4, 4) time(s), working last 2 sts of each RS row as p1, k1—13 (13, 14, 14, 16, 16) sts total removed at neck edge.

At the same time, when piece measures 15 (15, 14¼, 14¼, 13½, 13½)" (38 [38, 36, 36, 34.5, 34.5] cm) from pick-up row and about 17½" (44.5 cm) from edging lower selvedge, shape armhole as foll: BO 4 (4, 4, 6, 6, 6) sts at the beg of the next RS row, then BO 2 (3, 3, 3, 4, 4) sts at the beg of the foll RS row, then BO 0 (2, 2, 2, 3, 3) sts at the beg of the next 0 (1, 2, 2, 1, 2) RS row(s), then BO 0 (0, 0, 0, 2, 2) sts at the beg of the foll 0 (0, 0, 0, 2, 3) RS rows, then dec 1 st at beg of next 4 (3, 4, 4, 3, 2) RS rows—10 (12, 15, 17, 20, 24) sts total removed at armhole edge; 10 (12, 12, 14, 13, 13) sts rem when all armhole and neck shaping is complete.

Work even until armhole measures 7 (7½, 8, 8½, 9, 9½)" (18 [19, 20.5, 21.5, 23, 24] cm), ending with a WS row.

Shape Shoulder

At armhole edge (beg of RS rows) BO 3 (3, 3, 4, 4, 4) sts once, then BO 3 (3, 3, 4, 3, 3) sts once, then BO 2 (3, 3, 3, 3, 3) sts 2 times—no sts rem.

Right Front

CO and work as for left front to start of armhole and neck shaping, ending with a WS row—33 (37, 41, 45, 49, 53) sts; piece measures 13½ (13½, 12¾, 12¾, 12, 12)" (34.5 [34.5, 32.5, 32.5, 30.5, 30.5] cm) from pick-up row and about 16" (40.5 cm) from edging lower selvedge for all sizes.

Shape Armhole and Neck

Note: *As for left front, armhole shaping begins while neck shaping is in progress; read all the way through the foll section before proceeding.*

Neck dec row: (RS) K1, p2tog, work in patt to end—1 st dec'd.

Rep neck dec row every 4th row 7 (9, 10, 12, 11, 11) more times, then every other row 5 (3, 3, 1, 4, 4) time(s), working last 2 sts of each WS row as p1, k1—13 (13, 14, 14, 16, 16) sts total removed at neck edge.

At the same time, when piece measures 15 (15, 14¼, 14¼, 13½, 13½)" (38 [38, 36, 36, 34.5, 34.5] cm) from pick-up row and about 17½" (44.5 cm) from edging lower selvedge, shape armhole as foll: BO 4 (4, 4, 6, 6, 6) sts at the beg of the next WS row, then BO 2 (3, 3, 3, 4, 4) sts at the beg of the foll WS row, then BO 0 (2, 2, 2, 3, 3) sts at the beg of the next 0 (1, 2, 2, 1, 2) WS row(s), then BO 0 (0, 0, 0, 2, 2) sts at the beg of the foll 0 (0, 0, 0, 2, 3) WS rows, then dec 1 st at end of next 4 (3, 4, 4, 3, 2) RS rows—10 (12, 15, 17, 20, 24) sts total removed at armhole edge; 10 (12, 12, 14, 13, 13) sts rem when all armhole and neck shaping is complete.

Work even until armhole measures 7 (7½, 8, 8½, 9, 9½)" (18 [19, 20.5, 21.5, 23, 24] cm), ending with a RS row.

Shape Shoulder
At armhole edge (beg of WS rows) BO 3 (3, 3, 4, 4, 4) sts once, then BO 3 (3, 3, 4, 3, 3) sts once, then BO 2 (3, 3, 3, 3, 3) sts 2 times—no sts rem.

Sleeves

With CC and larger needle, CO 19 sts for all sizes. Do not join.

Rep edging Rows 1 and 2 as for back until piece measures 8 (8½, 9, 9½, 10, 10)" (20.5 [21.5, 23, 24, 25.5, 25.5] cm) from CO, ending with a WS row. BO all sts.

With MC, smaller needle, and RS facing, pick up and knit 34 (36, 38, 40, 43, 43) sts evenly spaced along garter selvedge of edging piece. Do not join.

Work even in seed st until piece measures 1" (2.5 cm) from pick-up row and about 3½" (9 cm) from edging lower selvedge, ending with a WS row.

Cont in patt, inc 1 st each end of needle on next RS row, then every 12 (8, 8, 8, 8, 6)th row 6 (1, 4, 9, 7, 3) more time(s), then every 0 (10, 10, 10, 10, 8)th row 0

(7, 5, 1, 3, 9) time(s), incorporating new sts into seed st patt—48 (54, 58, 62, 65, 69) sts.

Work even until piece measures 15 (15, 15½, 15½, 16, 16)" (38 [38, 39.5, 39.5, 40.5, 40.5] cm) from pick-up row and about 17½ (17½, 18, 18, 18½, 18½)" (44.5 [44.5, 45.5, 45.5, 47, 47] cm) from edging lower selvedge, ending with a WS row.

Shape Cap
BO 4 (4, 4, 6, 6, 6) sts at the beg of the next 2 rows—40 (46, 50, 50, 53, 57) sts rem.

BO 2 sts at the beg of the next 2 rows, then BO 1 st at the beg of the foll 4 (12, 12, 10, 14, 16) rows—32 (30, 34, 36, 35, 37) sts rem.

[BO 1 st at beg of next 2 rows, then work 2 rows even] 4 (3, 3, 4, 4, 4) times—24 (24, 28, 28, 27, 29) sts rem.

BO 1 st at beg of next 2 (2, 4, 4, 2, 2) rows, then BO 2 sts at beg of foll 4 rows—14 (14, 16, 16, 17, 19) sts rem.

BO all sts.

Finishing

Pockets (make 2)

With MC and smaller cir needle, CO 20 (20, 24, 24, 28, 28) sts. Do not join.

Work in seed st until piece measures 6" (15 cm) from CO for all sizes.

BO all sts.

Elbow Patches (make 2)

With MC and smaller cir needle, CO 6 sts. Do not join.

Work 2 rows even in seed st.

CO 2 sts at the beg of the next 2 rows—10 sts.

Inc 1 stitch each end of needle every RS row 3 times, incorporating new sts into seed st patt—16 sts.

Work even in patt until piece measures 4" (10 cm) from CO.

Keeping in patt, dec 1 st each end of needle every RS row 3 times—10 sts rem.

BO 2 sts at beg of next 2 rows—6 sts rem.

Work 2 rows even—piece measures about 5½" (14 cm) from CO.

BO all sts.

Block body pieces to measurements shown on schematic. Block each pocket to 4¾ (4¾, 5¾, 5¾, 6½, 6½)" (12 [12, 14.5, 14.5, 16.5, 16.5] cm) wide and 6" (15 cm) high.

Block each elbow patch to 3¾" (9.5 cm) wide and 5½" (14 cm) high.

With just MC threaded on a tapestry needle, sew shoulder seams. Sew side and sleeve seams. Sew sleeve caps into armholes, matching center of cap BO with shoulder seam and matching sleeve seam with side seam at underarm.

Place a pocket on each front, centered between the side seam and front edge so that the CO edge of pocket is aligned with the pick-up row. With just MC threaded on a tapestry needle, sew pocket in place around three sides, leaving top open.

Try on cardigan, bend your arms, and mark the center of your elbow point on the RS of each sleeve. Place an elbow patch on each sleeve, matching the middle of the patch with the elbow point so that the vertical stitch columns of the patch and sleeve are aligned. With just MC threaded on a tapestry needle, sew all the way around each patch.

Front Bands and Collar

With removable markers, mark position of 6 buttonholes on right front, the lowest ¾" (2 cm) up from the lower selvedge of edging, the highest ¼" (6 mm) below the start of the V-neck shaping, and the other 4 evenly spaced in between.

With CC, smaller needle, RS facing, and beg at lower selvedge of edging, pick up and knit 81 sts evenly spaced along right front edge to the beg of the V-neck shaping, place marker (pm), 45 (50, 50, 55, 55, 55) sts evenly spaced along right front neck to shoulder seam, pm, 41 (41, 46, 46, 51, 51) sts evenly spaced across back neck, pm, 45 (50, 50, 55, 55, 55) sts evenly spaced along left front neck to base of V-neck, pm, and 81 sts evenly spaced along left front edge to end at lower selvedge of edging—293 (303, 308, 318, 323, 323) sts total.

Row 1: (WS) P3, *k2, p3; rep from *.

Row 2: (RS) K3, *p2, k3; rep from*.

Row 3: Rep Row 1.

Row 4: Work in rib as established, working a ([yo] 2 times, k2tog) buttonhole at each marked position.

Row 5: Work in rib as established, dropping the extra yo in each buttonhole. Remove buttonhole markers.

Row 6: Rep Row 2.

Work short-rows (see Glossary) to shape shawl collar as foll.

Short-Row 1: (WS) Work in rib patt along left front, left neck, back, and right neck to 5 sts before marker at base of right V-neck, wrap next st and turn work (w&t).

Short-Row 2: (RS) Work in rib patt along right neck, back, and left neck to 5 sts before marker at base of left V-neck, w&t.

Short-Rows 3 and 4: Work in rib patt to 5 sts before previously wrapped st, w&t.

Rep Short-Rows 3 and 4 only 10 (11, 12, 12, 13, 13) more times—12 (13, 14, 14, 15, 15) wrapped sts at each side; 11 (11, 6, 16, 11, 11) sts between last pair of wrapped sts at back neck.

Next 2 rows: Work in rib patt to end of row, working wraps tog with wrapped sts when you come to them.

Cont in rib as established until band measures 2" (5 cm) from pick-up row along front edges (outside first and last short-row markers)—collar measures about 5¾ (6, 6¼, 6¼, 6½, 6½)" (14.5 [15, 16, 16, 16.5, 16.5] cm) from pick-up row at center back.

BO all sts in patt.

Weave in loose ends. Sew buttons to left front band opposite buttonholes.

Montmartre

intarsia scoop-neck pullover

Finished Size
About 33½ (37, 40½, 45, 49, 53)" (85 [94, 103, 114.5, 124.5, 134.5] cm) bust circumference.

Designed to be worn with about 1" (2.5 cm) of positive ease.

Pullover shown measures 37" (94 cm).

Yarn
Sportweight (#2 Fine).

Shown here: Jamieson's of Shetland Spindrift (100% Shetland wool; 115 yd [105 m]/25 g): #127 Pebble (MC, light gray), 7 (8, 9, 10, 11, 12) balls; #123 Oxford (CC1, dark gray), 4 (5, 5, 6, 6, 7) balls; #595 Maroon (CC2), 1 ball for all sizes.

Needles
Body and sleeves: size U.S. 3 (3.25 mm): straight or circular (cir).

Ribbing: size U.S. 1½ (2.5 mm): straight or cir.

Neckband: size U.S. 1½ (2.5 mm): 16" (40 cm) cir.

Adjust needle size if necessary to obtain the correct gauge.

Notions
Markers (m); yarn bobbins; tapestry needle.

Gauge
25 sts and 37 rows = 4" (10 cm) in St st intarsia patts from charts with larger needles.

This close-fitting pullover is worked in four pieces (back, front, and two sleeves) that are seamed together. The neck is shaped with a deep U in the front and a subtle dip in the back for a comfortable fit. Intarsia heart motifs add allover femininity.

When working the charted stockinette intarsia pattern, use a separate length of yarn for each color section. This includes the sections of main background color between the hearts, which should not be stranded across the back of the heart motifs.

Wrap lengths of yarn on bobbins for ease of use.

Twist yarns around each other at color changes to prevent holes from forming.

Refer to Chapter 1 for general knitting foundations.

Back

With CC1 and smaller needles, CO 112 (124, 138, 152, 166, 178) sts.

Next row: (RS) *K1, p1; rep from *.

Cont in k1, p1 rib (knit the knits and purl the purls) for 1 more row. Change to MC and cont in rib until piece measures 1¾" (4.5 cm) from CO, ending with a WS row.

Change to larger needles and St st (knit RS rows; purl WS rows).

Next row: (RS) Knit and *at the same time* dec 8 (9, 11, 12, 13, 13) sts evenly spaced—104 (115, 127, 140, 153, 165) sts rem.

Purl 1 WS row.

Set-up row: (RS) Using a separate length of yarn for each color section (see Notes), k5 (1, 7, 4, 4, 10) with MC, place marker (pm), work Row 1 of Montmartre Chart B (A, A, B, A, A) over center 94 (113, 113, 132, 145, 145) sts, pm, k5 (1, 7, 4, 4, 10) with MC.

Note: *After working Rows 1–18 of the chart for your size once, repeat Rows 19–54 for the pattern; do not work Rows 1–18 again.*

Working sts outside chart at each end of row in St st with MC, cont as established until piece measures 15" (38 cm) from CO for all sizes, ending with a WS row.

Shape Armholes

Cont in patt, BO 5 (5, 5, 7, 7, 7) sts at the beg of the next 2 (2, 4, 2, 2, 4) rows, then BO 3 (3, 3, 5, 5, 5) sts at the beg of the foll 2 (4, 2, 2, 4, 4) rows—88 (93, 101, 116, 119, 117) sts rem.

Sizes 45 (49, 53)" (114.5 [124.5, 134.5] cm) only

BO 3 sts at the beg of the next 2 (4, 2) rows—110 (107, 111) sts rem.

All sizes

Dec 1 st at each armhole edge every RS row 6 (6, 7, 8, 6, 8) times—76 (81, 87, 94, 95, 95) sts rem.

Work even until armholes measure 7 (7½, 8, 8½, 9, 9½)" (18 [19, 20.5, 21.5, 23, 24] cm), ending with a WS row.

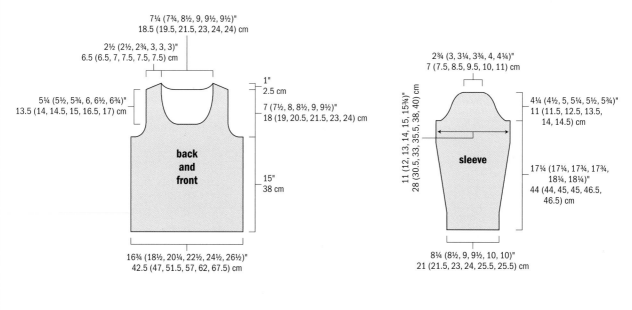

7¼ (7¾, 8½, 9, 9½, 9½)"
18.5 (19.5, 21.5, 23, 24, 24) cm

2½ (2½, 2¾, 3, 3, 3)"
6.5 (6.5, 7, 7.5, 7.5, 7.5) cm

5¼ (5½, 5¾, 6, 6½, 6¾)"
13.5 (14, 14.5, 15, 16.5, 17) cm

1"
2.5 cm

7 (7½, 8, 8½, 9, 9½)"
18 (19, 20.5, 21.5, 23, 24) cm

15"
38 cm

back and front

16¾ (18½, 20¼, 22½, 24½, 26½)"
42.5 (47, 51.5, 57, 62, 67.5) cm

2¾ (3, 3¼, 3¾, 4, 4¼)"
7 (7.5, 8.5, 9.5, 10, 11) cm

11 (12, 13, 14, 15, 15¾)"
28 (30.5, 33, 35.5, 38, 40) cm

4¼ (4½, 5, 5¼, 5½, 5¾)"
11 (11.5, 12.5, 13.5, 14, 14.5) cm

17¼ (17¼, 17¾, 17¾, 18¼, 18¼)"
44 (44, 45, 45, 46.5, 46.5) cm

sleeve

8¼ (8½, 9, 9½, 10, 10)"
21 (21.5, 23, 24, 25.5, 25.5) cm

Shape Neck and Shoulders

Note: *Neck and shoulders are shaped at the same time; read all the way through the next section before proceeding.*

Keeping in patt, work 26 (28, 31, 33, 33, 33) sts, join new ball of yarn and BO 24 (25, 25, 28, 29, 29) center sts, work to end—26 (28, 31, 33, 33, 33) sts rem each side.

Working each side separately, at each armhole edge BO 4 (4, 5, 5, 5, 5) sts once, then BO 4 (4, 4, 5, 5, 5) sts once, then BO 4 (4, 4, 5, 4, 4) sts once, then BO 3 (4, 4, 4, 4, 4) sts once and *at the same time* at each neck edge BO 6 (6, 7, 7, 7, 7) sts once, then BO 5 (6, 7, 7, 8, 8) sts once— no sts rem.

MONTMARTRE CHART A

53
51
49
47
45
43
41
39
repeat for pattern
37
35
33
31
29
27
25
23
21
19
17
15
13
11
work once
9
7
5
3
1

☐ MC

☒ CC1

☐ pattern repeat

Front

Work as for back until 108 chart rows have been completed, ending with Row 36 of chart—104 (115, 127, 140, 153, 165) sts; piece measures about 13¾" (35 cm) from CO.

Next row: (RS; Row 37 of chart) Work in patt, and substitute CC2 for the second heart motif from beg of the row as shown in the photographs, or for the heart that begins in this row that will sit closest to your actual heart (alternatively, you can work all hearts in CC1, then cover the selected heart with CC2 duplicate sts once the knitting is complete); work all other heart motifs in CC1 as before.

Cont as established until piece measures 15" (38 cm) from CO for all sizes, ending with a WS row.

Shape Armholes

Work as for back, then work 1 WS row even after the last armhole dec row—76 (81, 87, 94, 95, 95) sts rem; armholes measure 1¾ (2, 2¼, 2½, 2½, 2¾)" (4.5 [5, 5.5, 6.5, 6.5, 7] cm).

Shape Neck

Keeping in patt, work 30 (31, 34, 37, 37, 37) sts, join new ball of yarn and BO 16 (19, 19, 20, 21, 21) center sts, work to end—30 (31, 34, 37, 37, 37) sts rem each side.

Working each side separately, at each neck edge BO

MONTMARTRE CHART B

53, 51, 49, 47, 45, 43, 41, 39, 37, 35, 33, 31, 29, 27, 25, 23, 21, 19, 17, 15, 13, 11, 9, 7, 5, 3, 1

repeat for pattern

work once

6 sts once, then 4 sts 1 (1, 1, 1, 2, 2) time(s), then BO 2 sts 1 (1, 2, 2, 1, 1) time(s), then BO 1 st 3 (3, 3, 3, 4, 3, 3) times—15 (16, 17, 19, 18, 18) sts rem. Work even until armholes measure 7 (7½, 8, 8½, 9, 9½)" (18 [19, 20.5, 21.5, 23, 24] cm), ending with a WS row.

Shape Shoulders

Working each side separately, at each armhole edge BO 4 (4, 5, 5, 5, 5) sts once, then BO 4 (4, 4, 5, 5, 5) sts once, then BO 4 (4, 4, 5, 4, 4) sts once, then BO 3 (4, 4, 4, 4, 4) sts once—no sts rem.

Sleeves

With CC1 and smaller needles, CO 54 (58, 60, 64, 68, 68) sts.

Next row: (RS) *K1, p1; rep from *.

Work in k1, p1 rib for 1 more row. Change to MC and cont in rib until piece measures 1¾" (4.5 cm) from CO, ending with a WS row.

Change to larger needles and St st.

Next row: (RS) Knit and *at the same time* dec 3 (5, 3, 5, 5, 5) sts evenly spaced—51 (53, 57, 59, 63, 63) sts rem.

Purl 1 WS row.

Set-up row: (RS) Using a separate length of yarn for each color section, k1 (2, 4, 5, 7, 7) with MC, pm,

MONTMARTRE CHART C

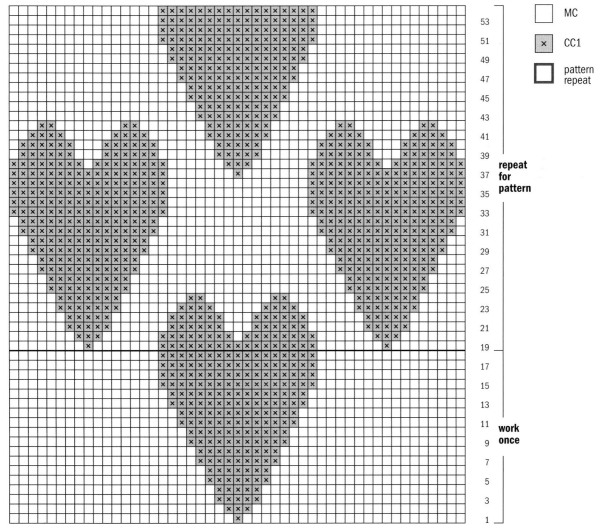

work Row 1 of Montmartre Chart C over center 49 sts, pm, k1 (2, 4, 5, 7, 7) with MC.

Note: *After working Rows 1–18 of Chart C once, repeat Rows 19–54 for the pattern; do not work Rows 1–18 again.*

Working sts outside chart at each end of row in St st with MC, work 9 (7, 5, 5, 5, 3) rows even, ending with a WS row.

Inc row: (RS) K1, M1 (see Glossary), work in patt to last st, M1, k1—2 sts inc'd.

Rep inc row every 12 (10, 8, 8, 8, 6)th row 8 (10, 1, 11, 14, 10) more time(s), then every 0 (0, 10, 10, 0, 8)th row 0 (0, 10, 2, 0, 7) times, working new sts in St st with MC (do not add any new heart motifs)—69 (75, 81, 87, 93, 99) sts.

Work even until piece measures 17¼ (17¼, 17¾, 17¾, 18¼, 18¼)" (44 [44, 45, 45, 46.5, 46.5] cm) from CO, ending with a WS row.

Shape Cap
BO 5 (5, 5, 7, 7, 7) sts at beg of next 2 rows—59 (65, 71, 73, 79, 85) sts rem.

BO 2 sts at beg of next 2 (4, 4, 2, 4, 4) rows, then BO 1 st at beg of the foll 12 (12, 16, 20, 20, 24) rows—43 (45, 47, 49, 51, 53) sts rem.

[BO 1 st at beg of next 2 rows, then work 2 rows even] 4 times—35 (37, 39, 41, 43, 45) sts rem.

BO 1 st at beg of next 2 rows, then BO 2 sts at beg of foll 2 rows, then BO 3 sts at beg of next 4 rows—17 (19, 21, 23, 25, 27) sts rem.

BO all sts.

Finishing

Block to measurements. With yarn threaded on a tapestry needle, sew side seams. Sew shoulder seams. Sew sleeve seams. Sew sleeve caps into armholes, matching center of cap BO with shoulder seam and matching sleeve seam with side seam at underarm.

Neckband
With MC, 16" (40 cm) cir needle in smaller size, RS facing, and beg at right shoulder seam, pick up and knit 52 (56, 60, 62, 66, 66) sts evenly spaced across back neck edge to left shoulder seam, then 102 (112, 118, 126, 134, 134) sts evenly spaced along front neck edge—154 (168, 178, 188, 200, 200) sts total.

Place marker (pm) and join for working in rnds.

Next rnd: *K1, p1; rep from *.

Rep the last rnd until neckband measures 1½" (3.8 cm).

Change to CC1 and work in rib for 2 more rnds.

With CC1, BO all sts in rib patt.

Weave in loose ends.

Chapter 4

Night

When designing for nighttime, I was drawn to fabrics that had a little extra sparkle, as well as to shapes that accentuate the contours of a woman's body. Although sweaters aren't typically worn on a night out, I designed these pullovers so that they could easily be dressed up. The sweaters in this chapter will make those around you wish they had worn one on their dates, too.

The *Eveleigh Sleeveless Cowl-Neck Pullover* and the *Xian Lace Pullover* (pages 84 and 96, respectively) are the dressiest of the sweaters in this chapter. Both designs feature sheer fabric at the upper bust, which makes them ultra sexy without actually revealing anything. The back button detail of the Eveleigh and the ornate lace pattern of the Xian add visual appeal, as well as interesting knitting. A simple, yet unexpected way to wear these sweaters for a night out is to tuck them into a pencil skirt.

The idea for the *Branford Beaded Dolman Pullover* (page 102) arose during hours of watching the show, *Mad Men*. I love how Betty Draper is styled. From her perfectly coiffed hair to her impeccably put-together outfits, Betty embodies what we think of today as vintage chic. I wanted to design something that Betty would wear out to dinner on a cool New York evening but that would still look appropriate today. Branford's classic dolman shape, combined with a chic beaded detail along the sleeves, achieves that look.

The *Salzburg Cabled Raglan Pullover* (page 108) is an updated take on a traditional fisherman's sweater. The wide boat neck and metallic yarn modernize this well-loved classic. Cables help to give the appearance of shaping without the necessity for increases or decreases. Mirrored cables on the raglan-shaped sleeves tie this whole piece together.

Inspired by 1960s mod fashion, the *Catalunya Funnel-Neck Pullover* (page 116) may be my favorite piece in this book. The funnel neck, paired with three-quarter-length sleeves, channels the timelessness of Audrey Hepburn, while the metallic textured fabric makes Catalunya a perfect choice for date night. Wear it with a pair of trim cigarette pants and ballet flats for a playful evening look.

Eveleigh

sleeveless cowl-neck pullover

Finished Size

About 33 (37, 41, 45, 49, 53)" (84 [94, 104, 114.5, 124.5, 134.5] cm) bust circumference and 27½ (31, 35½, 39, 43, 47½)" (70 [79, 90, 99, 109, 120.5] cm) waist circumference.

Designed to be worn with 1" (2.5 cm) of positive ease.

Pullover shown measures 33" (84 cm) bust circumference.

Yarn

Worsted weight (#4 Medium) and laceweight (#0 Lace).

Shown here: Cascade Venezia Worsted (70% merino wool, 30% silk; 219 yd [200 m]/100 g): #159 Ruby (MC), 3 (4, 4, 5, 5, 5) skeins.

Cascade Alpaca Lace (100% baby alpaca; 437 yd [400 m]/50 g): #1415 Red Wine Heather (CC), 1 (2, 2, 2, 2, 2) skein(s).

Needles

Upper body stockinette: size U.S. 6 (4 mm): straight or 24" (60 cm) or longer circular (cir).

Lower body rib: size U.S. 5 (3.75 mm): straight or 24" (60 cm) or longer cir.

Sheer upper body and collar: size U.S. 4 (3.5 mm): 16" and 24" (40 and 60 cm) cir.

Adjust needle size if necessary to obtain the correct gauge.

Notions

Markers (m); removable markers; tapestry needle; 3 (3, 3, 4, 4, 4) ⅝" (1.5 cm) buttons.

Gauge

20 sts and 28 rows = 4" (10 cm) in St st with MC on largest needles.

26 sts and 30 rows = 4" (10 cm) in k2, p1 rib (slightly stretched) with MC on middle-size needles.

28 sts and 44 rows = 4" (10 cm) in St st with CC on smallest needles.

This close-fitting sleeveless pullover is the ultimate in elegant wear, whether it's for day or night. The ribbed lower body and stockinette bust are worked in a luxurious silk/wool blend, while the upper bodice and generous cowl collar are worked in lacy baby alpaca. A few buttons at the back add functional allure.

Refer to Chapter 1 for general knitting foundations.

Back

With MC and middle-size needles, CO 108 (120, 135, 147, 159, 174) sts.

Next row: (RS) *K2, p1; rep from *.

Work sts as they appear (knit the knits, and purl the purls) for 2" (5 cm), ending with a WS row.

Shape Waist

Note: New markers are added every decrease row and will be used to indicate locations for increasing later.

Dec Row 1: (RS) K2, p1, pm, k2tog, work in established rib to last 3 sts, pm, k2tog, p1—2 sts dec'd.

Work 3 rows even, working sts as they appear.

Dec Row 2: (RS) K2, p1, slip marker (sl m) k1, p1, k2, p1, pm, k2tog, work to last 8 sts, pm, k2tog, p1, k2, p1, sl m, k1, p1—2 sts dec'd.

Work 3 rows even.

Dec Row 3: (RS) K2, p1, [sl m, k1, p1, k2, p1] 2 times, pm, k2tog, work to last 13 sts, pm, k2tog, p1, k2, p1, sl m, k1, p1, k2, p1, sl m, k1, p1—2 sts dec'd.

Work 3 rows even.

Dec Row 4: (RS) K2, p1, [sl m, k1, p1, k2, p1] 3 times, pm, k2tog, work to 6 sts before next m, pm, k2tog, p1, k2, p1, [sl m, k1, p1, k2, p1] 2 times, sl m, k1, p1—2 sts dec'd.

Work 3 rows even.

Dec Row 5: (RS) K2, p1, [sl m, k1, p1, k2, p1] 4 times, pm, k2tog, work to 6 sts before next m, pm, k2tog, p1, k2, p1, [sl m, k1, p1, k2, p1] 3 times, sl m, k1, p1—2 sts dec'd.

Note: To continue the decreases in this manner, work each section in [ ] one additional time on each successive decrease row.

[Work 3 rows even, then work a dec row] 4 (5, 5, 5, 5, 5) times, ending with a RS dec row—90 (100, 115, 127, 139, 154) sts rem; 9 (10, 10, 10, 10, 10) markers on each side of center; piece measures 6½ (7, 7, 7, 7, 7)" (16.5 [18, 18, 18, 18, 18] cm) from CO.

Work even until piece measures 8½" (21.5 cm) from CO for all sizes, ending with a WS row.

Inc Row 1: (RS) Work in patt to 9 (10, 10, 10, 10, 10)th m, M1 (see Glossary), remove m, work in patt to next m, remove m, M1, work in patt to end—2 sts inc'd.

Work 3 rows even, incorporating new sts into the k2, p1 rib patt by working them as knit sts.

Inc Row 2: (RS) Work in patt to 8 (9, 9, 9, 9, 9)th m, remove m, M1, work in patt to next m, remove m,

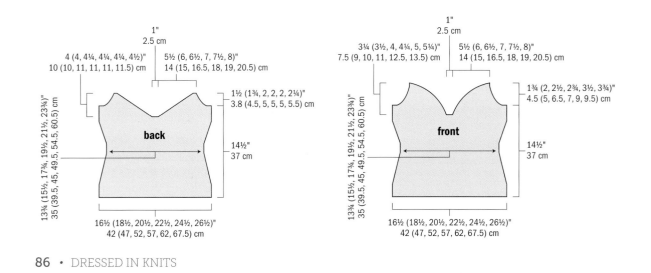

4 (4, 4¼, 4¼, 4¼, 4½)"
10 (10, 11, 11, 11, 11.5) cm

1"
2.5 cm

5½ (6, 6½, 7, 7½, 8)"
14 (15, 16.5, 18, 19, 20.5) cm

1½ (1¾, 2, 2, 2, 2¼)"
3.8 (4.5, 5, 5, 5, 5.5) cm

back

13¾ (15½, 17¾, 19½, 21½, 23¾)"
35 (39.5, 45, 49.5, 54.5, 60.5) cm

14½"
37 cm

16½ (18½, 20½, 22½, 24½, 26½)"
42 (47, 52, 57, 62, 67.5) cm

3¼ (3½, 4, 4¼, 5, 5¼)"
7.5 (9, 10, 11, 12.5, 13.5) cm

1"
2.5 cm

5½ (6, 6½, 7, 7½, 8)"
14 (15, 16.5, 18, 19, 20.5) cm

1¾ (2, 2½, 2¾, 3½, 3¾)"
4.5 (5, 6.5, 7, 9, 9.5) cm

front

13¾ (15½, 17¾, 19½, 21½, 23¾)"
35 (39.5, 45, 49.5, 54.5, 60.5) cm

14½"
37 cm

16½ (18½, 20½, 22½, 24½, 26½)"
42 (47, 52, 57, 62, 67.5) cm

M1, work in patt to end—2 sts inc'd.

Note: *To continue the increases in this manner, work to the last marker before the center stitches, remove the marker, M1, work to the first marker after the center stitches, remove the marker, M1, work to end.*

[Work 3 rows even, then work an inc row] 3 times, then work 3 rows even—100 (110, 125, 137, 149, 164) sts; 4 (5, 5, 5, 5, 5) markers rem at each side; piece measures 11¼" (28.5 cm) from CO.

Change to largest needles and St st.

Next row: (RS) Knit, removing all markers and *at the same time* dec 22 (24, 29, 31, 33, 38) sts evenly spaced—78 (86, 96, 106, 116, 126) sts rem.

Work 1 row even.

Inc row: (RS) K24 (24, 28, 28, 34, 34), M1, knit to last 24 (24, 28, 28, 34, 34) sts, M1, knit to end—2 sts inc'd.

Rep inc row every RS row 1 (2, 2, 2, 2, 2) more time(s), then work 1 WS row—82 (92, 102, 112, 122, 132) sts; piece measures 12 (12¼, 12¼, 12¼, 12¼, 12¼)" (30.5 [31, 31, 31, 31, 31] cm) from CO.

Shape Right Back, Left Back, and Armholes
Note: *The two back halves are worked at the same time and the armhole shaping is introduced during their shaping; read all the way through the following section before proceeding.*

Next row: (RS) K38 (43, 48, 53, 58, 63), join new yarn and BO 6 sts, knit to end—38 (43, 48, 53, 58, 63) sts rem each side.

Working each side separately, dec 1 st on each side of gap at center back every row 25 (28, 30, 33, 35, 38) times.

At the same time, when the piece measures 14½" (37 cm) from CO, shape armholes as foll. At each armhole edge, BO 4 (4, 4, 8, 8, 8) sts once, then BO 3 (3, 3, 3, 4, 3) sts 1 (1, 2, 1, 1, 3) time(s), then BO 2 (2, 2, 2, 3, 2) sts 1 (2, 2, 2, 1, 2) time(s), then BO 1 (1, 1, 1, 2, 1) st(s) 2 (2, 2, 3, 2, 2) times, then BO 0 (0, 0, 0, 1, 0) st 0 (0, 0, 0, 2, 0) times—2 sts rem each side when all back and armhole shaping is complete; armholes measure 1½ (1¾, 2, 2, 2, 2¼)" (3.8 [4.5, 5, 5, 5, 5.5] cm).

BO all sts.

Front

Work as for back to end of ribbed lower body—100 (110, 125, 137, 149, 164) sts; 4 (5, 5, 5, 5, 5) m rem at each side; piece measures 11¼" (28.5 cm) from CO.

Change to largest needles and St st.

Next row: (RS) Knit, removing rem markers and *at the same time* dec 22 (24, 29, 31, 33, 38) sts evenly spaced—78 (86, 96, 106, 116, 126) sts rem.

Work 1 row even.

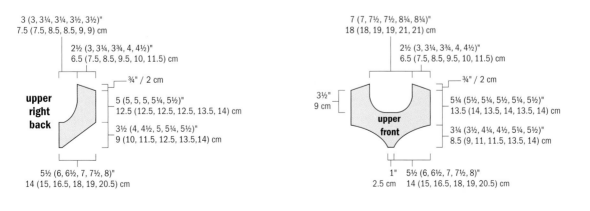

3 (3, 3¼, 3¼, 3½, 3½)"
7.5 (7.5, 8.5, 8.5, 9, 9) cm

2½ (3, 3¼, 3¾, 4, 4½)"
6.5 (7.5, 8.5, 9.5, 10, 11.5) cm

¾" / 2 cm

upper right back

5 (5, 5, 5, 5¼, 5½)"
12.5 (12.5, 12.5, 12.5, 13.5, 14) cm

3½ (4, 4½, 5, 5¼, 5½)"
9 (10, 11.5, 12.5, 13.5,14) cm

5½ (6, 6½, 7, 7½, 8)"
14 (15, 16.5, 18, 19, 20.5) cm

7 (7, 7½, 7½, 8¼, 8¼)"
18 (18, 19, 19, 21, 21) cm

2½ (3, 3¼, 3¾, 4, 4½)"
6.5 (7.5, 8.5, 9.5, 10, 11.5) cm

¾" / 2 cm

3½"
9 cm

upper front

5¼ (5½, 5¼, 5½, 5¼, 5½)"
13.5 (14, 13.5, 14, 13.5, 14) cm

3¼ (3½, 4¼, 4½, 5¼, 5½)"
8.5 (9, 11, 11.5, 13.5, 14) cm

1"
2.5 cm

5½ (6, 6½, 7, 7½, 8)"
14 (15, 16.5, 18, 19, 20.5) cm

Inc row: (RS) K16 (16, 19, 19, 22, 22), M1, knit to last 16 (16, 19, 19, 22, 22) sts, M1, knit to end—2 sts inc'd.

Rep inc row every RS row 1 (2, 2, 2, 2, 2) more time(s)—82 (92, 102, 112, 122, 132) sts.

Next row: (WS) P41 (46, 51, 56, 61, 66), pm at center, purl to end.

Work even until piece measures 13" (33 cm) from CO for all sizes, ending with a WS row.

Shape Left Bust and Armhole

Work short-rows (see Glossary) to shape left half of front (beg of RS rows; end of WS rows) as foll.

Short-Row 1: (RS) Knit to 4 sts before center m, wrap next st and turn work (w&t).

Even-Numbered Short-Rows 2–8: (WS) Purl to end.

Short-Row 3: Knit to 6 sts before center m, w&t.

Short-Row 5: Knit to 7 sts before center m, w&t.

Short-Row 7: Knit to 8 sts before center m, w&t.

Short-Row 9: Knit to 10 (10, 9, 9, 9, 9) sts before center m, w&t.

Short-Row 10: (WS) Purl to end—piece measures 14½" (37 cm) from CO along left side (beg of RS rows).

Beg shaping left armhole while cont short-rows as foll.

Short-Row 11: BO 4 (4, 4, 8, 8, 8) sts, knit to 11 (11, 10, 11, 10, 10) sts before center m, w&t—37 (42, 47, 48, 53, 58) sts rem.

Even-Numbered Short-Rows 12–18: Purl to end.

Short-Row 13: BO 3 (3, 3, 3, 4, 3) sts, knit to 12 sts before center m, w&t—34 (39, 44, 45, 49, 55) sts rem.

Short-Row 15: BO 2 (2, 3, 2, 3, 3) sts, knit to 13 (14, 13, 13, 13, 13) sts before center m, w&t—32 (37, 41, 43, 46, 52) sts rem.

Short-Row 17: BO 1 (2, 2, 2, 2, 3) st(s), knit to 14 (15, 14, 14, 14, 14) sts before center m, w&t—31 (35, 39, 41, 44, 49) sts rem.

Short-Row 19: BO 1 (1, 2, 1, 2, 2) st(s), knit to 16 (16, 15, 16, 15, 15) sts before center m, w&t—30 (34, 37, 40, 42, 47) sts rem.

Short-Row 20: Purl to end.

Cont for your size as foll.

Size 33" (84 cm) only
Armhole shaping is complete for this size.

Short-Row 21: Knit to 19 sts before center m, w&t.

Short-Row 22: Purl to end—armhole measures 1¾" (4.5 cm).

Size 37" (94 cm) only
Short-Row 21: BO 1 st, knit to 18 sts before center m, w&t—33 sts rem; armhole shaping is complete.

Short-Row 22: Purl to end.

Short-Row 23: Knit to 21 sts before center m, w&t.

Short-Row 24: Purl to end—armhole measures 2" (5 cm).

Size 41" (104 cm) only
Short-Row 21: BO 1 st, knit to 16 sts before center m, w&t—36 sts rem.

Even-Numbered Short-Rows 22–26: Purl to end.

Short-Row 23: BO 1 st, knit to 17 sts before center m, w&t—35 sts rem; armhole shaping is complete.

Short-Row 25: Knit to 19 sts before center m, w&t.

Short-Row 27: Knit to 22 sts before center m, w&t.

Short-Row 28: Purl to end—armhole measures 2½" (6.5 cm).

Size 45" (114.5 cm) only
Short-Row 21: BO 1 st, knit to 17 sts before center m, w&t—39 sts rem.

Even-Numbered Short-Rows 22–28: Purl to end.

Short-Row 23: BO 1 st, knit to 18 sts before center m, w&t—38 sts rem; armhole shaping is complete.

Short-Row 25: Knit to 19 sts before center m, w&t.

Short-Row 27: Knit to 21 sts before center m, w&t.

Short-Row 29: Knit to 24 sts before center m, w&t.

Short-Row 30: Purl to end—armhole measures 4¼" (11 cm).

Size 49" (124.5 cm) only
Short-Row 21: BO 1 st, knit to 16 sts before center m, w&t—41 sts rem.

Even-Numbered Short-Rows 22–32: Purl to end.

Short-Row 23: BO 1 st, knit to 18 sts before center m, w&t—40 sts rem; armhole shaping is complete.

Short-Row 25: Knit to 19 sts before center m, w&t.

Short-Row 27: Knit to 20 sts before center m, w&t.

Short-Row 29: Knit to 21 sts before center m, w&t.

Short-Row 31: Knit to 23 sts before center m, w&t.

Short-Row 33: Knit to 26 sts before center m, w&t.

Short-Row 34: Purl to end—armhole measures 3½" (9 cm).

Size 53" (134.5 cm) only
Short-Row 21: BO 2 sts, knit to 16 sts before center m, w&t—45 sts rem.

Even-Numbered Short-Rows 22–34: Purl to end.

Short-Row 23: BO 1 st, knit to 18 sts before center m, w&t—44 sts rem.

Short-Row 25: BO 1 st, knit to 19 sts before center m, w&t—43 sts rem; armhole shaping is complete.

Short-Row 27: Knit to 20 sts before center m, w&t.

Short-Row 29: Knit to 22 sts before center m, w&t.

Short-Row 31: Knit to 23 sts before center m, w&t.

Short-Row 33: Knit to 25 sts before center m, w&t.

Short-Row 35: Knit to 28 sts before center m, w&t.

Short-Row 36: Purl to end—armhole measures 3¾" (9.5 cm).

All sizes
Next row: (RS) Knit to center m, working wraps tog with wrapped sts, sl m, knit to end—30 (33, 35, 38, 40, 43) left front sts before m, 41 (46, 51, 56, 61, 66) right front sts after m.

Shape Right Bust and Armhole
Work short-rows to shape right half of front (beg of WS rows; end of RS rows) as foll.

Short-Row 1: (WS) Purl to 4 sts before center m, w&t.

Even-Numbered Short-Rows 2–8: (RS) Knit to end.

Short-Row 3: Purl to 6 sts before center m, w&t.

Short-Row 5: Purl to 7 sts before center m, w&t.

Short-Row 7: Purl to 8 sts before center m, w&t.

Short-Row 9: Purl to 10 (10, 9, 9, 9, 9) sts before center m, w&t.

Short-Row 10: Knit to end—piece measures 14½" (37 cm) from CO along right side (end of RS rows).

Beg shaping right armhole while cont short-rows as foll.

Short-Row 11: BO 4 (4, 4, 8, 8, 8) sts, purl to 11 (11, 10, 11, 10, 10) sts before center m, w&t—37 (42, 47, 48, 53, 58) sts rem.

Even-Numbered Short-Rows 12–18: Knit to end.

Short-Row 13: BO 3 (3, 3, 3, 4, 3) sts, purl to 12 sts before center m, w&t—34 (39, 44, 45, 49, 55) sts rem.

Short-Row 15: BO 2 (2, 3, 2, 3, 3) sts, purl to 13 (14, 13, 13, 13, 13) sts before center m, w&t—32 (37, 41, 43, 46, 52) sts rem.

Short-Row 17: BO 1 (2, 2, 2, 2, 3) st(s), purl to 14 (15, 14, 14, 14, 14) sts before center m, w&t—31 (35, 39, 41, 44, 49) sts rem.

Short-Row 19: BO 1 (1, 2, 1, 2, 2) st(s), purl to 16 (16, 15, 16, 15, 15) sts before center m, w&t—30 (34, 37, 40, 42, 47) sts rem.

Short-Row 20: Knit to end.

Cont for your size as foll.

Size 33" (84 cm) only
Armhole shaping is complete for this size.

Short-Row 21: Purl to 19 sts before center m, w&t.

Short-Row 22: Knit to end—armhole measures 1¾" (4.5 cm).

Size 37" (94 cm) only
Short-Row 21: BO 1 st, purl to 18 sts before center m, w&t—33 sts rem; armhole shaping is complete.

Short-Row 22: Knit to end.

Short-Row 23: Purl to 21 sts before center m, w&t.

Short-Row 24: Knit to end—armhole measures 2" (5 cm).

Size 41" (104 cm) only
Short-Row 21: BO 1 st, purl to 16 sts before center m, w&t—36 sts rem.

Even-Numbered Short-Rows 22–26: Knit to end.

Short-Row 23: BO 1 st, purl to 17 sts before center m, w&t—35 sts rem; armhole shaping is complete.

Short-Row 25: Purl to 19 sts before center m, w&t.

Short-Row 27: Purl to 22 sts before center m, w&t.

Short-Row 28: Knit to end—armhole measures 2½" (6.5 cm).

Size 45" (114.5 cm) only
Short-Row 21: BO 1 st, purl to 17 sts before center m, w&t—39 sts rem.

Even-Numbered Short-Rows 22–28: Knit to end.

Short-Row 23: BO 1 st, purl to 18 sts before center m, w&t—38 sts rem; armhole shaping is complete.

Short-Row 25: Purl to 19 sts before center m, w&t.

Short-Row 27: Purl to 21 sts before center m, w&t.

Short-Row 29: Purl to 24 sts before center m, w&t.

Short-Row 30: Knit to end—armhole measures 2¾" (7.5 cm).

Size 49" (124.5 cm) only
Short-Row 21: BO 1 st, purl to 16 sts before center m, w&t—41 sts rem.

Even-Numbered Short-Rows 22–32: Knit to end.

Short-Row 23: BO 1 st, purl to 18 sts before center m, w&t—40 sts rem; armhole shaping is complete.

Short-Row 25: Purl to 19 sts before center m, w&t.

Short-Row 27: Purl to 20 sts before center m, w&t.

Short-Row 29: Purl to 21 sts before center m, w&t.

Short-Row 31: Purl to 23 sts before center m, w&t.

Short-Row 33: Purl to 26 sts before center m, w&t.

Short-Row 34: Knit to end—armhole measures 3½" (9 cm).

Size 53" (134.5 cm) only
Short-Row 21: BO 2 sts, purl to 16 sts before center m, w&t—45 sts rem.

Even-Numbered Short-Rows 22–34: Knit to end.

Short-Row 23: BO 1 st, purl to 18 sts before center m, w&t—44 sts rem.

Short-Row 25: BO 1 st, purl to 19 sts before center m, w&t—43 sts rem; armhole shaping is complete.

Short-Row 27: Purl to 20 sts before center m, w&t.

Short-Row 29: Purl to 22 sts before center m, w&t.

Short-Row 31: Purl to 23 sts before center m, w&t.

Short-Row 33: Purl to 25 sts before center m, w&t.

Short-Row 35: Purl to 28 sts before center m, w&t.

Short-Row 36: Knit to end—armhole measures 3¾" (9.5 cm).

All sizes
Next row: (WS) Purl to center m, working wraps tog with wrapped sts, remove m, purl to end—60 (66, 70, 76, 80, 86) sts rem.

With RS facing, BO all sts.

Sheer upper right back

With CC and either cir needle in smallest size, CO 3 sts.

Purl 1 WS row.

Work in St st for your size as foll, using the backward-loop method (see Glossary) to CO sts and the M1 method to inc sts.

Size 33" (84 cm) only
[CO 2 sts at the beg of the next 5 RS rows, then inc 1 st at the beg of the foll RS row] 3 times—36 sts.

CO 2 sts at the beg of the next RS row—38 sts; piece measures 3½" (9 cm).

Size 37" (94 cm) only
[CO 2 sts at the beg of the next 3 RS rows, then inc 1 st at the beg of the foll RS row] 5 times—38 sts.

CO 2 sts at the beg of the next 2 RS rows—42 sts; piece measures 4" (10 cm).

Size 41" (104 cm) only
[CO 2 sts at the beg of the next 2 RS rows, then inc 1 st at the beg of the foll RS row] 7 times—38 sts.

CO 2 sts at the beg of the next 4 RS rows—46 sts; piece measures 4½" (11.5 cm).

Size 45" (114.5 cm) only
[CO 2 sts at the beg of the next 4 RS rows, then inc 1 st at the beg of the foll RS row] 5 times—48 sts.

CO 1 st at the beg of the next RS row—49 sts; piece measures 5" (12.5 cm).

Size 49" (124.5 cm) only
[CO 2 sts at the beg of the next 2 RS rows, then inc 1 st at the beg of the foll RS row] 9 times—48 sts.

CO 2 sts at the beg of the next 2 RS rows—52 sts; piece measures 5¼" (13.5 cm).

Size 53" (134.5 cm) only

[CO 2 sts at the beg of the next 3 RS rows, then inc 1 st at the beg of the foll RS row] 7 times—52 sts.

CO 2 sts at the beg of the next 2 RS rows—56 sts; piece measures 5½" (14 cm).

Shape Neck

At neck edge (beg of WS rows), BO 5 (5, 6, 5, 5, 6) sts once, then BO 6 sts once, then BO 3 sts 1 (1, 2, 2, 2, 2) time(s), then BO 2 sts 2 (2, 1, 1, 2, 2) time(s), then BO 1 st 3 (3, 4, 4, 3, 3) times—17 (21, 22, 26, 28, 31) sts rem.

Work even until piece measures 8½ (9, 9½, 10, 10½, 11)" (21.5 [23, 24, 25.5, 26.5, 28] cm) from initial CO, ending with a WS row.

Shape Shoulder

At armhole edge (beg of RS rows), BO 4 (5, 5, 6, 7, 7) sts once, then BO 4 (5, 5, 6, 7, 8) sts once, then BO 4 (5, 6, 7, 7, 8) sts once, then BO 5 (6, 6, 7, 7, 8) sts once—no sts rem.

Sheer upper left back

With CC and either cir needle in smallest size, CO 3 sts.

Knit 1 RS row.

Work in St st for your size as foll, using the backward-loop method to CO sts and the M1P (see Glossary) method to inc sts.

Size 33" (84 cm) only

[CO 2 sts at the beg of the next 5 WS rows, then inc 1 st at the beg of the foll WS row] 3 times—36 sts.

CO 2 sts at the beg of the next WS row—38 sts; piece measures 3½" (9 cm).

Size 37" (94 cm) only

[CO 2 sts at the beg of the next 3 WS rows, then inc 1 st at the beg of the foll WS row] 5 times—38 sts.

CO 2 sts at the beg of the next 2 WS rows—42 sts; piece measures 4" (10 cm).

Size 41" (104 cm) only

[CO 2 sts at the beg of the next 2 WS rows, then inc 1 st at the beg of the foll WS row] 7 times—38 sts.

CO 2 sts at the beg of the next 4 WS rows—46 sts; piece measures 4½" (11.5 cm).

Size 45" (114.5 cm) only

[CO 2 sts at the beg of the next 4 WS rows, then inc 1 st at the beg of the foll WS row] 5 times—48 sts.

CO 1 st at the beg of the next WS row—49 sts; piece measures 5" (12.5 cm).

Size 49" (124.5 cm) only

[CO 2 sts at the beg of the next 2 WS rows, then inc 1 st at the beg of the foll WS row] 9 times—48 sts.

CO 2 sts at the beg of the next 2 WS rows—52 sts; piece measures 5¼" (13.5 cm).

Size 53" (134.5 cm) only

[CO 2 sts at the beg of the next 3 WS rows, then inc 1 st at the beg of the foll WS row] 7 times—52 sts.

CO 2 sts at the beg of the next 2 WS rows—56 sts; piece measures 5½" (14 cm).

Shape Neck

At neck edge (beg of RS rows), BO 5 (5, 6, 5, 5, 6) sts once, then BO 6 sts once, then BO 3 sts 1 (1, 2, 2, 2, 2) time(s), then BO 2 sts 2 (2, 1, 1, 2, 2) time(s), then BO 1 st 3 (3, 4, 4, 3, 3) times—17 (21, 22, 26, 28, 31) sts rem each side.

Work even until piece measures 8½ (9, 9½, 10, 10½, 11)" (21.5 [23, 24, 25.5, 26.5, 28] cm) from initial CO, ending with a RS row.

Shape Shoulder

At armhole edge (beg of WS rows), BO 4 (5, 5, 6, 7, 7) sts once, then BO 4 (5, 5, 6, 7, 8) sts once, then BO 4 (5, 6, 7, 7, 8) sts once, then BO 5 (6, 6, 7, 7, 8) sts once—no sts rem.

Sheer upper front

With CC and either cir needle in smallest size, CO 7 sts.

Purl 1 WS row.

Work in St st for your size as foll, using the backward-loop method to CO sts and using the M1 method to inc sts on RS rows and the M1P method to inc sts on WS rows.

Size 33" (84 cm) only
[CO 2 sts at the beg of the next 2 rows, then inc 1 st at the beg of the foll 4 rows] 5 times—47 sts.

Inc 1 st at the beg of the next 4 rows—51 sts.

CO 16 sts at the beg of the next 2 rows—83 sts; piece measures 3¼" (8.5 cm).

Size 37" (94 cm) only
[CO 2 sts at the beg of the next 2 rows, then inc 1 st at the beg of the foll 2 rows] 8 times—55 sts.

Inc 1 st at the beg of the next 4 rows—59 sts.

CO 16 sts at the beg of the next 2 rows—91 sts; piece measures 3½" (9 cm).

Size 41" (104 cm) only
[CO 2 sts at the beg of the next 2 rows, then inc 1 st at the beg of the foll 8 rows] 4 times—55 sts.

Inc 1 st at the beg of the next 4 rows—59 sts.

CO 19 sts at the beg of the next 2 rows—97 sts; piece measures 4¼" (11 cm).

Size 45" (114.5 cm) only
[CO 2 sts at the beg of the next 2 rows, then inc 1 st at the beg of the foll 6 rows] 5 times—57 sts.

Inc 1 st at the beg of the next 6 rows—63 sts.

CO 21 sts at the beg of the next 2 rows—105 sts; piece measures 4½" (11.5 cm).

Size 49" (124.5 cm) only
[CO 2 sts at the beg of the next 2 rows, then inc 1 st at the beg of the foll 12 rows] 4 times—71 sts.

CO 21 sts at the beg of the next 2 rows—113 sts; piece measures 5¼" (13.5 cm).

Size 53" (134.5 cm) only
[CO 2 sts at the beg of the next 2 rows, then inc 1 st at the beg of the foll 6 rows] 6 times—67 sts.

Inc 1 st at the beg of the next 10 rows—77 sts.

CO 21 sts at the beg of the next 2 rows—119 sts; piece measures 5½" (14 cm).

All Sizes
Work even until piece measures 5 (5½, 6, 6½, 7, 7½)" (12.5 [14, 15, 16.5, 18, 19] cm) from initial CO, ending with a WS row.

Shape Neck
Next row: (RS) K33 (37, 40, 44, 47, 50), join new yarn and BO center 17 (17, 17, 17, 19, 19) sts, knit to end—33 (37, 40, 44, 47, 50) sts rem each side.

Working each side separately, at each neck edge BO 6 sts once, then BO 3 sts 1 (1, 2, 2, 2, 2) time(s), then BO 2 sts 2 (2, 1, 1, 2, 2) time(s), then BO 1 st 3 (3, 4, 4, 3, 3) times—17 (21, 22, 26 28, 31) sts rem each side.

Work even until piece measures 8½ (9, 9½, 10, 10½, 11)" (21.5 [23, 24, 25.5, 26.5, 28] cm) from initial CO, ending with a WS row.

Shape Shoulders
At each armhole edge BO 4 (5, 5, 6, 7, 7) sts once, then BO 4 (5, 5, 6, 7, 8) sts once, then BO 4 (5, 6, 7, 7, 8) sts once, then BO 5 (6, 6, 7, 7, 8) sts once—no sts rem.

Finishing

Block pieces to measurements.

Note: The upper left back is not shown on the schematic; block it into a mirror-image of the upper right back piece.

Pin RS of each sheer piece's lower edge to WS of each MC piece's upper edge so that MC fabric slightly overlaps CC fabric, leaving a 1" (2.5 cm) gap between upper back pieces at center back for button placket. With CC threaded on a tapestry needle, use a running-stitch seam (see Glossary) to sew pieces tog.

With MC threaded on a tapestry needle, sew front and back side seams. With CC threaded on a tapestry needle, sew shoulder seams.

Armhole Edging

With CC and shorter needle in smallest size, pick up and knit 84 (90, 96, 102, 108, 114) sts evenly spaced around armhole opening. Place marker (pm) and join for working in rnds.

Next rnd: *K1, p1; rep from *.

Rep the last rnd until edging measures 1" (2.5 cm).

BO all sts in patt.

Buttonband

With CC, smallest needles, and RS facing, pick up and knit 21 (24, 27, 29, 32, 33) sts evenly spaced along right back placket edge.

Work in St st until piece measures 1" (2.5 cm) from pick-up row, ending with a RS row.

Next row: (WS) Purl for fold line, working each st through the back loop.

Work in St st until piece measures 1" (2.5 cm) from fold line.

Fold band to WS along fold-line ridge and, with yarn threaded on a tapestry needle, sew live sts carefully to WS of pick-up row.

Buttonhole Band

Mark placement of 3 (3, 3, 4, 4, 4) buttonholes on left back placket edge, the highest ½" (1.3 cm) below neck edge, the lowest ½" (1.3 cm) up from base of placket opening, and the others evenly spaced between.

With CC, smallest needles, and RS facing, pick up and knit 21 (24, 27, 29, 32, 33) sts evenly spaced along left back placket edge.

Work in St st until piece measures ½" (1.3 cm) from pick-up row, ending with a WS row.

Buttonhole row: (RS) Knit, working a ([yo] 2 times, k2tog) buttonhole at each marked buttonhole position.

Dropping the extra yo wrap on the foll row, cont in St st until band measures 1" (2.5 cm) from pick-up row, ending with a RS row.

Next row: (WS) Purl for fold line, working each st through the back loop.

Work in St st until piece measures ½" (1.3 cm) from fold line, ending with a WS row.

Buttonhole row: (RS) Knit, working a ([yo] 2 times, k2tog) buttonhole directly above each buttonhole in the first half of the band.

Dropping the extra yo wrap on the foll row, cont in St st until band measures 1" (2.5 cm) from fold line.

Fold band to WS along fold-line ridge and, with yarn threaded on a tapestry needle, sew live sts carefully to WS of pick-up row.

With CC threaded on a tapestry needle, work buttonhole st (see Glossary) to join the two layers of each buttonhole opening.

Sew buttons to buttonband opposite buttonholes. With CC threaded on a tapestry needle, sew short edges of buttonband and buttonhole band to base of placket, sewing through all layers.

Collar

Note: Collar is worked in the round with a steek (see Steeks, page 20), then cut open to make a flat rectangle.

With CC and longer cir needle in smallest size, CO 238 (238, 252, 252, 266, 266) sts.

Pm and join for working in rnds, being careful not to twist sts.

Next rnd: P7 for steek, knit to end.

Next rnd: K7 for steek, knit to end.

Rep the last 2 rnds until piece measures 5" (12.5 cm) from CO.

BO all sts as foll: K2, *insert left needle tip from left to right into the front 2 sts on right needle, k2tog through their back loops, k1; rep from * until 1 st rem, then fasten off last st.

Mark and secure fabric on each side of 7-st garter steek, then cut piece open along center of steek as described on page 20.

Fold raw edges of steek to WS about ¼" (6 mm),

then fold once more to cover the raw edge, and sew in place. Block collar into a rectangle about 34 (34, 36, 36, 38, 38)" (86.5 [86.5, 91.5, 91.5, 96.5, 96.5] cm) wide and 5" (12.5 cm) high.

Turn garment inside out. Pin collar to neck edge between pick-up rows of back placket bands (collar does not extend across top of bands), easing to fit, and with RS of collar corresponding to WS of garment so the RS of collar will show on outside when collar is folded back. With CC threaded on a tapestry needle, use running sts to seam pieces tog.

Weave in loose ends.

Xian

lace pullover

Finished Size

About 33 (37, 41, 45, 49, 53)" (84 [94, 104, 114.5, 124.5, 134.5] cm) bust circumference.

Designed to be worn with 1" (2.5 cm) of positive ease.

Pullover shown measures 33" (84 cm).

Yarn

DK weight (#3 Light) and fingering weight (#1 Super Fine).

Shown here: Malabrigo Silky Merino (50% silk, 50% merino wool; 150 yd [137 m]/50 g): #431 Tatami (MC; gold), 4 (4, 5, 5, 6, 6) skeins.

Cascade Heritage Silk (85% merino wool, 15% mulberry silk; 437 yd [400 m]/100 g): #5672 Real Black (CC), 1 (1, 1, 2, 2, 2) skein(s).

Needles

Body and sleeves: size U.S. 6 (4 mm): straight or 24" (60 cm) or longer circular (cir).

Ribbing: size U.S. 4 (3.5 mm): straight or 24" (60 cm) or longer cir.

Adjust needle size if necessary to obtain the correct gauge.

Notions

Tapestry needle; stitch holder; size G/6 (4.25 mm) crochet hook.

Gauge

22 sts and 32 rows = 4" (10 cm) in St st with MC on larger needles.

19 sts and 28 rows = 4" (10 cm) in lace patt from Chart A or Chart B with single strand of CC on larger needles, after blocking.

This close-fitting pullover is worked in pieces from the bottom to the top. It features a feminine lace pattern throughout the yoke that reveals a modest amount of skin. The contrasting color of the lace yoke is repeated at the cast-on edges for a polished look.

notes

The cast-on and first two rows of ribbing are worked with two strands of the contrasting color held together. The lace pattern of the upper body and upper sleeves is worked using a single strand of the contrasting color.

During shaping, if there are not enough stitches in the lace pattern to work each yarnover with its companion decrease, work the stitches in stockinette instead.

Refer to Chapter 1 for general knitting foundations.

Back

With 2 strands of CC held tog and smaller needles, CO 99 (111, 123, 135, 147, 159) sts.

Next row: (RS) *K2, p1; rep from *.

Work sts as they appear (knit the knits, and purl the purls) for 1 WS row.

Change to MC and cont in established rib until piece measures 1" (2.5 cm) from CO, ending with a WS row.

Change to larger needles.

Next row: (RS) Knit and *at the same time* dec 8 (9, 10, 11, 12, 13) sts evenly spaced—91 (102, 113, 124, 135, 146) sts rem.

Work even in St st (knit RS rows; purl WS rows) until piece measures 13½" (34.5 cm) from CO for all sizes, ending with a RS row.

Change to a single strand of CC.

Next row: (WS) Purl and *at the same time* dec 16 (15, 20, 19, 18, 23) sts evenly spaced—75 (87, 93, 105, 117, 123) sts rem.

Next row: (RS) K1 (selvedge st; knit every row), work Xian Chart A (A, B, B, B, A) over next 73 (85, 91, 103, 115, 121) sts, k1 (selvedge st; knit every row).

Cont in patt as established until piece measures 14½" (37 cm) from CO for all sizes, ending with a WS row.

Shape Armholes

Note: *During the foll shaping, BO in lace patt as foll: K2, *insert left needle tip from left to right into the fronts of 2 sts on right needle tip, k2tog through back loops (tbl), k1; rep from * until the required number of sts has been bound off.*

Keeping in patt (see Notes on page 97) and using the lace patt method described above, BO 4 (4, 4, 6, 6, 7) sts at the beg of the next 2 rows, then BO 2 (2, 2, 4, 4, 4) sts at the beg of the foll 2 (4, 4, 2, 4, 4) rows—63 (71, 77, 85, 89, 93) sts rem.

BO 1 (1, 1, 2, 2, 2) st(s) at the beg of the next 8 (8, 8, 6, 6, 6) rows, then BO 0 (0, 0, 1, 1, 1) st at the beg of the

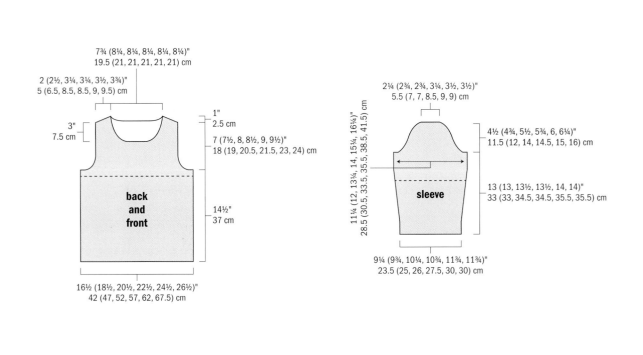

foll 0 (0, 0, 2, 4, 6) rows—55 (63, 69, 71, 73, 75) sts rem.

Work even in patt until armholes measure 7 (7½, 8, 8½, 9, 9½)" (18 [19, 20.5, 21.5, 23, 24] cm), ending with a WS row.

Shape Neck and Shoulders

BO 2 (3, 4, 4, 5, 5) sts st the beg of the next 2 rows—51 (57, 61, 63, 63, 65) sts rem.

Next row: (RS) BO 2 (3, 4, 4, 4, 5) sts, work in patt until there are 14 (16, 17, 18, 18, 18) sts on right needle, join new ball of yarn and BO 19 center sts, work in patt to end—14 (16, 17, 18, 18, 18) sts rem for right shoulder; 16 (19, 21, 22, 22, 23) sts rem for left shoulder.

Place 14 (16, 17, 18, 18, 18) right shoulder sts onto holder.

Left Shoulder

Cont on left shoulder sts only as foll.

Next row: (WS) BO 2 (3, 4, 4, 4, 5) sts, work in patt to end—14 (16, 17, 18, 18, 18) sts rem.

Next row: (RS) BO 5 sts at neck edge, work in patt to end—9 (11, 12, 13, 13, 13) sts rem.

Next row: BO 2 (3, 4, 4, 4, 4) sts, work in patt to end—7 (8, 8, 9, 9, 9) sts rem.

Next row: BO 4 (5, 5, 5, 5, 5) sts at neck edge, work in patt to end—3 (3, 3, 4, 4, 4) sts rem.

BO all sts.

Right Shoulder

With WS facing, return 14 (16, 17, 18, 18, 18) held right shoulder sts to larger needle.

Next row: (WS) BO 5 sts at neck edge, work in patt to end—9 (11, 12, 13, 13, 13) sts rem.

Next row: (RS) BO 2 (3, 4, 4, 4, 4) sts, work in patt to end—7 (8, 8, 9, 9, 9) sts rem.

Next row: BO 4 (5, 5, 5, 5, 5) sts at neck edge, work in patt to end—3 (3, 3, 4, 4, 4) sts rem.

BO all sts.

---

	knit on RS; purl on WS	○	yo
/	k2tog		pattern repeat
\	ssk		

CHART A

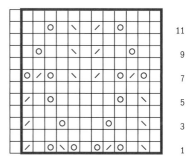

12-st repeat

CHART B

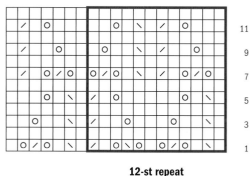

12-st repeat

Front

CO and work as for back until armhole shaping has been completed—55 (63, 69, 71, 73, 75) sts rem.

Work even in patt until armholes measure 4 (4½, 5, 5½, 6, 6½)" (10 [11.5, 12.5, 14, 15, 16.5] cm), ending with a WS row.

Shape Neck

With RS facing, work 21 (25, 28, 29, 30, 31) sts in patt, join new ball of yarn and BO 13 sts in lace patt, work in patt to end—21 (25, 28, 29, 30, 31) sts rem each side.

Working each side separately, at each neck edge BO 4 sts once, then BO 3 sts once, then BO 2 sts once, then BO 1 st 3 (4, 4, 4, 4, 4) times—9 (12, 15, 16, 17, 18) sts rem each side.

Work even in patt until armholes measure 7 (7½, 8, 8½, 9, 9½)" (18 [19, 20.5, 21.5, 23, 24] cm), ending with a WS row.

Shape Shoulders

At each armhole edge, BO 2 (3, 4, 4, 5, 5) sts once, then BO 2 (3, 4, 4, 4, 5) sts once, then BO 2 (3, 4, 4, 4, 4) sts once, then BO 3 (3, 3, 4, 4, 4) sts once—no sts rem.

Sleeves

With 2 strands of CC held tog and smaller needles, CO 54 (57, 63, 66, 72, 72) sts.

Next row: (RS) *K2, p1; rep from *.

Work sts as they appear for 1 WS row.

Change to MC and cont in established rib until piece measures 1" (2.5 cm) from CO, ending with a WS row.

Change to larger needles.

Next row: (RS) Knit and *at the same time* dec 3 (3, 7, 7, 7, 8) sts evenly spaced—51 (54, 56, 59, 65, 64) sts rem.

Work even in St st (knit RS rows; purl WS rows) until piece measures 5 (2, 2, 2, 2, 2)" (12.5 [5, 5, 5, 5, 5] cm) from CO, ending with a WS row.

Inc row: (RS) K1, M1 (see Glossary), knit to last st, M1, k1—2 sts inc'd.

Rep inc row every 0 (10, 10, 10, 10, 8) rows 0 (3, 1, 3, 1, 2) more time(s), then every 0 (0, 8, 0, 8, 6) rows 0 (0, 4, 0, 4, 5) times, working new sts in St st—53 (62, 68, 67, 77, 80) sts.

Work even until piece measures 8½" (21.5 cm) from CO, ending with a RS row.

Change to a single strand of CC.

Next row: (WS) Purl and *at the same time* dec 8 (11, 11, 10, 14, 11) sts evenly spaced—45 (51, 57, 57, 63, 69) sts rem.

Next row: (RS) K1 (selvedge st; knit every row), M1, work Chart B (A, B, B, A, B) over center 43 (49, 55, 55, 61, 67) sts, M1, k1 (selvedge st; knit every row)—2 sts inc'd.

Inc 1 st at each side as in the previous row every 6 (6, 6, 4, 4, 4) rows 3 (2, 2, 2, 4, 3) more times, then every 0 (0, 0, 4, 0, 0) rows 0 (0, 0, 2, 0, 0) more times, incorporating new sts into chart patt—53 (57, 63, 67, 73, 77) sts.

Work even in patt until piece measures 13 (13, 13½, 13½, 14, 14)" (33 [33, 34.5, 34.5, 35.5, 35.5] cm) from CO, ending with a WS row.

Shape Cap
Binding off in lace patt as for back and front armholes, BO 4 (4, 4, 6, 6, 7) sts at the beg of the next 2 rows—45 (49, 55, 55, 61, 63) sts rem.

Dec 1 st at each end of needle every RS row 13 (14, 15, 12, 15, 16) times—19 (21, 25, 31, 31, 31) sts rem.

Dec 1 st at each end of needle every 4th row (i.e., every other RS row) 0 (0, 0, 2, 1, 1) time(s)—19 (21, 25, 27, 29, 29) sts rem.

BO 2 sts at the beg of the next 4 (4, 6, 6, 6, 6) rows— 11 (13, 13, 15, 17, 17) sts rem.

BO all sts.

Finishing

Block pieces to measurements.

With coordinating yarn threaded on a tapestry needle, sew side seams. Sew shoulder seams. Sew sleeve seams. Sew sleeve caps into armholes, matching center of cap BO with shoulder seam and matching sleeve seam with side seam at underarm.

Neck Edging
With a single strand of CC and crochet hook, work 1 row of single crochet (see Glossary) around neck edge.

Weave in loose ends.

Branford

beaded dolman pullover

Finished Size
About 36½ (40½, 44½, 48½, 52½, 56½)" (92.5 [103, 113, 123, 133.5, 143.5] cm) bust circumference and 32½ (37, 40½, 45, 48½, 53)" (82.5 [94, 103, 114.5, 123, 134.5] cm) hip circumference.

Designed to be worn with about 4" to 5" (10 to 12.5 cm) of positive ease at the bust.

Pullover shown measures 36½" (92.5 cm) at bust.

Yarn
DK weight (#3 Light).

Shown here: Madelinetosh Tosh DK (100% superwash merino wool; 225 yd [206 m]/ 120 g): Betty Draper's Blue, 5 (5, 6, 7, 7, 8) skeins.

Needles
Body and Sleeves: size U.S. 6 (4 mm): 32" (80 cm) or longer circular (cir).

Ribbing: size U.S. 4 (3.5 mm): 16" and 24" (40 and 60 cm) circular (cir).

Adjust needle size if necessary to obtain the correct gauge.

Notions
Stitch marker (m); removable markers or waste yarn; stitch holders; tapestry needle; 40 (45, 50, 55, 60, 65) grams size 6/0 seed beads in an assortment of pearlescent, crystal, and matte finishes to coordinate with yarn color; sewing thread to match yarn color; sharp-point sewing needle.

Gauge
22 sts and 28 rows = 4" (10 cm) in St st on larger needles.

This dolman-style pullover begins with stitches cast on for the lower front, which is worked up to the armholes, then stitches are cast on for both sleeves. The body and sleeves continue over the shoulders—with the neck shaped along the way—and back down to the armholes, at which point the sleeve stitches are bound off and the body continues to the lower back. After a couple of seams, cuffs, and a neckband are worked, beads are attached for a little glam along the sleeves.

Circular needles are used to accommodate the large number of stitches when the sleeves are included; do not join for working in rounds.

The right sleeve is not shown on the schematic; its dimensions are the same as for the left sleeve.

The ribbed cuffs applied during finishing are also not shown on the schematic for blocking purposes. The cuffs will add 3½" (9 cm) to the length of each sleeve.

Refer to Chapter 1 for general knitting foundations.

Front

With longer cir needle in smaller size, CO 93 (105, 117, 129, 141, 153) sts. Do not join.

Next row: (RS) *K2, p1; rep from *.

Cont in k2, p1 rib (knit the knits and purl the purls) until piece measures 4" (10 cm) from CO, ending with a WS row.

Change to larger cir needle and St st.

Next row: (RS) Knit and *at the same time* dec 3 (3, 5, 5, 7, 7) sts evenly spaced—90 (102, 112, 124, 134, 146) sts rem.

Work even until piece measures 5" (12.5 cm) from CO, ending with a WS row.

Inc row: (RS) K1, M1 (see Glossary), knit to last st, M1, k1—2 sts inc'd.

[Work 7 rows even, then rep the inc row] 2 times, working new sts in St st—96 (108, 118, 130, 140, 152) sts.

[Work 9 rows even, then rep the inc row] 2 times—100 (112, 122, 134, 144, 156) sts.

Work even until piece measures 11½ (11¼, 11, 10¾, 10¾, 10¾)" (29 [28.5, 28, 27.5, 27.5, 27.5] cm) from CO, ending with a WS row.

Shape Sleeves

Inc row: (RS) K1, M1, knit to last st, M1, k1— 2 sts inc'd.

Rep inc row every RS row 3 more times, then work 1 WS row after last inc row—108 (120, 130, 142, 152, 164) sts. Using the backward-loop method (see Glossary), CO 2 sts at the beg of the next 4 rows, then CO 3 sts at the beg of the foll 2 rows—122 (134, 144, 156, 166, 178) sts.

Using the backward-loop method, CO 4 sts at the beg of the next 6 rows, then CO 56 (56, 59, 59, 62, 62) sts at the beg of the foll 2 rows—258 (270, 286, 298, 314, 326) sts; piece measures 14¾ (14½, 14¼, 14, 14, 14)" (37.5 [37, 36, 35.5, 35.5, 35.5] cm) from CO.

Mark each end of last row completed with waste yarn or removable markers to indicate start of cuff opening.

Divide for Right and Left Front

With RS facing, k129 (135, 143, 149, 157, 163) for left front, join new ball of yarn, ssk, k127 (133, 141, 147, 155, 161), then place 128 (134, 142, 148, 156, 162) right front sts just worked onto holder—129 (135, 143, 149, 157, 163) left front sts rem on needle.

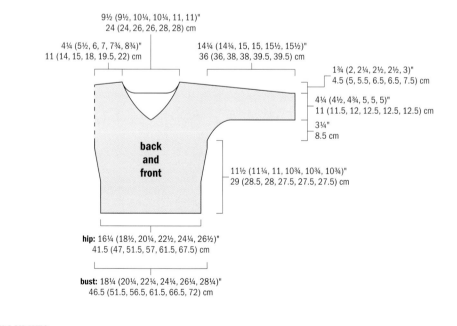

9½ (9½, 10¼, 10¼, 11, 11)"
24 (24, 26, 26, 28, 28) cm

4¼ (5½, 6, 7, 7¾, 8¾)"
11 (14, 15, 18, 19.5, 22) cm

14¼ (14¼, 15, 15, 15½, 15½)"
36 (36, 38, 38, 39.5, 39.5) cm

1¾ (2, 2¼, 2½, 2½, 3)"
4.5 (5, 5.5, 6.5, 6.5, 7.5) cm

4¼ (4½, 4¾, 5, 5, 5)"
11 (11.5, 12, 12.5, 12.5, 12.5) cm

3¼"
8.5 cm

back and front

11½ (11¼, 11, 10¾, 10¾, 10¾)"
29 (28.5, 28, 27.5, 27.5, 27.5) cm

hip: 16¼ (18½, 20¼, 22½, 24¼, 26½)"
41.5 (47, 51.5, 57, 61.5, 67.5) cm

bust: 18¼ (20¼, 22¼, 24¼, 26¼, 28¼)"
46.5 (51.5, 56.5, 61.5, 66.5, 72) cm

Shape Left Front Neck and Shoulder

Note: *Short-rows (see Glossary) are introduced to raise the shoulder line while neck shaping is in progress; read all the way through the following sections before proceeding so you do not accidentally work past the point where the short-rows should begin.*

Dec row: (WS) P2tog, purl to end, or to short-row turning point as required—1 st dec'd.

[Work 1 RS row even, then rep the dec row] 9 (9, 11, 11, 13, 13) times, then work 1 RS row—119 (125, 131, 137, 143, 149) sts rem.

At neck edge (beg of WS rows), BO 2 sts 1 (1, 0, 0, 1, 1) time, then BO 2 sts every 4th row 1 (1, 8, 8, 7, 7) time(s)—115 (121, 115, 121, 127, 133) sts rem.

[BO 2 sts at neck edge on next WS row, work 1 RS row even, BO 2 sts at neck edge on foll WS row, then work 3 rows even] 3 (3, 0, 0, 0, 0) times—103 (109, 115, 121, 127, 133) sts rem.

Work even at neck edge until short-rows have been completed.

At the same time, when piece measures 4 (4¼, 4½, 4¾, 4¾, 4¾)" (10 [11, 11.5, 12, 12, 12] cm) from marked row at start of cuff opening, work short-rows (see Glossary) to shape shoulder as foll.

Short-Row 1: (WS) Including any required neck shaping, purl to last 7 (6, 6, 5, 5, 5) sts, wrap next st and turn work (w&t).

Short-Row 2: (RS) Knit to end.

Short-Row 3: Including any required neck shaping, purl to 7 (6, 6, 5, 5, 5) sts before previous wrapped st, w&t.

Short-Row 4: Knit to end.

Rep the last 2 short-rows 9 (10, 12, 14, 14, 17) more times—11 (12, 14, 16, 16, 19) wrapped sts; last wrapped st is the 77th (72nd, 84th, 80th, 80th, 95th) st from cuff edge (beg of RS rows).

Next row: (WS) Including any required neck shaping, purl to end, working wraps tog with wrapped sts.

Work 1 RS row even—short-row section contains 24 (26, 30, 34, 34, 40) rows at neck edge and 2 rows at cuff edge (beg of RS rows); piece measures 4¼ (4½, 4¾, 5, 5, 5)" (11 [11.5, 12, 12.5, 12.5, 12.5] cm) from marked row at cuff edge and 6 (6½, 7, 7½, 7½, 8)" (15 [16.5, 18, 19, 19, 20.5] cm) from marked row to mid-point of short-row section (12 [13, 15, 17, 17, 20] rows from start of short-rows). Mark the mid-point of short-row section at neck edge for shoulder line.

Shape Left Back Neck

Use the backward-loop method to CO 6 (6, 7, 7, 7, 7) sts at beg of next WS row, work 1 RS row, then CO 7 (7, 7, 7, 8, 8) sts at beg of next WS row—116 (122, 129, 135, 142, 148) sts. Place sts onto holder; do not break yarn at cuff edge.

Shape Right Front Neck and Shoulder

Note: *As for left front, short-rows are introduced while neck shaping is in progress; read all the way through the following sections before proceeding.*

Return 128 (134, 142, 148, 156, 162) held right front sts onto larger needle. Turn work so WS is facing and use yarn attached at end of last RS row to purl 1 WS row.

Dec row: (RS) Ssk, knit to end, or to short-row turning point as required—1 st dec'd.

[Work 1 WS row even, then rep the dec row] 8 (8, 10, 10, 12, 12) times—119 (125, 131, 137, 143, 149) sts rem.

At neck edge (beg of RS rows), BO 2 sts 1 (1, 0, 0, 1, 1) time, then BO 2 sts every 4th row 1 (1, 8, 8, 7, 7) time(s)—115 (121, 115, 121, 127, 133) sts rem.

Work even at neck edge until short-rows have been completed.

[BO 2 sts at neck edge on next RS row, work 1 WS row even, BO 2 sts at neck edge on foll RS row, then work 3 rows even] 3 (3, 0, 0, 0, 0) times—103 (109, 115, 121, 127, 133) sts rem.

At the same time, when piece measures 4 (4¼, 4½, 4¾, 4¾, 4¾)" (10 [11, 11.5, 12, 12, 12] cm) from marked row at start of cuff opening, work short-rows to shape shoulder as foll.

Short-Row 1: (RS) Including any required neck shaping, knit to last 7 (6, 6, 5, 5, 5) sts, w&t.

Short-Row 2: (WS) Purl to end.

Short-Row 3: Including any required neck shaping, knit to 7 (6, 6, 5, 5, 5) sts before previous wrapped st, w&t.

Short-Row 4: Purl to end.

Rep the last 2 short-rows 9 (10, 12, 14, 14, 17) more times—11 (12, 14, 16, 16, 19) wrapped sts; last wrapped st is the 77th (72nd, 84th, 80th, 80th, 95th) st from cuff edge (end of RS rows).

Next row: (RS) Including any required neck shaping, knit to end, working wraps tog with wrapped sts.

Work 1 WS row even—piece measures 4¼ (4½, 4¾, 5, 5, 5)" (11 [11.5, 12, 12.5, 12.5, 12.5] cm) from marked row at cuff edge and 6 (6½, 7, 7½, 7½, 8)" (15 [16.5, 18, 19, 19, 20.5] cm) from marked row to mid-point of short-row section (12 [13, 15, 17, 17, 20] rows from start of short-rows). Mark the mid-point of short-row section at neck edge for shoulder line.

Shape Right Back Neck
Use the backward-loop method to CO 6 (6, 7, 7, 7, 7) sts at beg of next RS row, work 1 WS row, CO 7 (7, 7, 7, 8, 8) sts at beg of next RS row, then work 1 WS row even—116 (122, 129, 135, 142, 148) sts. Place sts onto holder and break yarn, leaving a 6" (15 cm) tail.

Back
. . . .
With RS facing, return 116 (122, 129, 135, 142, 148) held left front sts to larger needle so they will be worked first on the next RS row.

Next row: (RS) K116 (122, 129, 135, 142, 148), use the backward-loop method to CO 26 (26, 28, 28, 30, 30) center back sts, k116 (122, 129, 135, 142, 148)—258 (270, 286, 298, 314, 326) sts total.

Work even in St st until piece measures 6 (6½, 7, 7½, 7½, 8)" (15 [16.5, 18, 19, 19, 20.5] cm) from marked shoulder line at neck edge, ending with a WS row.

Shape Sleeves
BO 56 (56, 59, 59, 62, 62) sts at the beg of the next 2 rows, then BO 4 sts at the beg of the foll 6 rows—122 (134, 144, 156, 166, 178) sts rem.

BO 3 sts at the beg of the next 2 rows, then BO 2 sts at the beg of the foll 4 rows—108 (120, 130, 142, 152, 164) sts rem.

Dec row: (RS) Ssk, work to last 2 sts, k2tog—2 sts dec'd.

Rep dec row every RS row 3 more times—100 (112, 122, 134, 144, 156) sts rem.

Work even until piece measures 10½ (10¾, 11, 11¼, 11¼, 11¾)" (26.5 [27.5, 28, 28.5, 28.5, 30] cm) from marked shoulder line at neck edges, ending with a WS row.

Rep dec row—2 sts dec'd.

[Work 9 rows even, rep dec row] 2 times—94 (106, 116, 128, 138, 150) sts rem.

[Work 7 rows even, rep dec row] 2 times—90 (102, 112, 124, 134, 146) sts rem.

Work even until piece measures 16¾ (17, 17¼, 17½, 17½, 18)" (42.5 [43, 44, 44.5, 44.5, 45.5] cm) from marked shoulder line at neck edge, ending with a RS row.

Next row: Purl and *at the same time* inc 3 (3, 5, 5, 7, 7) sts evenly spaced—93 (105, 117, 129, 141, 153) sts.

Change to longer cir needle in smaller size and work in k2, p1 rib for 4" (10 cm), ending with a WS row—piece measures 20¾ (21, 21¼, 21½, 21½, 22)" (52.5 [53.5, 54, 54.5, 54.5, 56] cm) from shoulder line at high point of neck edge.

BO all sts in rib patt.

Finishing

Block to measurements (see Notes). With yarn threaded on a tapestry needle, sew front to back along sleeve and side seams.

Cuffs
With shorter cir needle in smaller size, pick up and knit 51 (54, 57, 60, 60, 60) sts evenly spaced around sleeve opening. Work in k2, p1 rib for 3½" (9 cm).

BO all sts in rib patt.

Neckband
With shorter cir needle in smaller size, RS facing, and beg at base of V at center front, pick up and knit 46 (50, 54, 58, 62, 66) sts evenly spaced along right front neck, 56 (56, 60, 60, 64, 64) sts evenly spaced across back neck, and 44 (48, 52, 56, 60, 62) sts evenly spaced along left front neck—146 (154, 166, 174, 186, 192) sts total.

Place marker (pm) and join for working in rnds.

Rnd 1: *K1, p1; rep from *.

Rnd 2: K1, k2tog, p1, *k1, p1; rep from * to last 2 sts, k2tog—2 sts dec'd.

Rnd 3: K2, p1 *k1, p1; rep from * to last st, k1.

Rnd 4: K1, k2tog, *k1, p1; rep from * to last 3 sts, k1, k2tog—2 sts dec'd.

Rnd 5: K2, *k1, p1; rep from * to last 2 sts, k2.

Rnd 6: K1, k2tog, p1, *k1, p1; rep from * to last 2 sts, k2tog—2 sts dec'd.

Rnd 7: K2, p1, *k1, p1; rep from * to last st, k1.

Rnd 8: K1, k2tog, *k1, p1; rep from * to last 3 sts, k1, k2tog—2 sts dec'd.

Rnd 9: K2, *k1, p1; rep from * to last 2 sts, k2.

Rnd 10: K1, k2tog, p1, *k1, p1; rep from * to last 2 sts, k2tog—2 sts dec'd.

Rnd 11: K2, p1 *k1, p1; rep from * to last st, k1.

Rnd 12: K1, k2tog, *k1, p1; rep from * to last 3 sts, k1, k2tog—2 sts dec'd.

Rnd 13: K2, *k1, p1; rep from * to last 2 sts, k2.

Rnd 14: K1, k2tog, p1, *k1, p1; rep from * to last 2 sts, k2tog—132 (140, 152, 160, 172, 178) sts rem.

BO all sts in rib patt.

Weave in loose ends.

Beaded Detail
Note: See Beads or Sequins on page 18.

With matching thread and sharp-point sewing needle, sew two lines of beads from neckband pick-up row to cuff pick-up row, each about 1" (2.5 cm) away from the fold along the top of the sleeve, with the beads in each line ⅜" (1 cm) to 1" (2.5 cm) apart. These lines mark two beaded areas 2" (5 cm) wide centered on the fold lines. Using sewing needle and thread, fill in the areas between the boundary lines with randomly chosen beads as shown, placing each bead at least ¼" (6 mm) away from its closest neighbors. As a general guideline, the pullover shown is the smallest size and about 175 beads were used in each area. However, your number may be different depending on your garment size and chosen bead placement.

Salzburg

cabled raglan pullover

Finished Size
About 35 (39, 43, 45, 49, 53)" (89 [99, 109, 114.5, 124.5, 134.5] cm) bust circumference.

Designed to be worn with 3" (7.5 cm) of positive ease at the bust.

Pullover shown measures 35" (89 cm).

Yarn
Worsted weight (#4 Medium) and sportweight (#2 Fine).

Shown here: Cascade Yarns Cascade 220 (100% Peruvian highland wool; 220 yd [200 m]/100 g): #8400 Charcoal Gray (MC), 6 (6, 7, 8, 8, 9) skeins.

Katia Yarns Gatsby (77% viscose, 15% nylon, 8% metallic polyester; 129 yd [118 m]/50 g): #7 Taupe/Silver (CC), 10 (11, 12, 13, 14, 15) balls.

Needles
Body and sleeves: size U.S. 7 (4.5 mm): straight or circular (cir) at least 32" (80 cm) long.

Ribbing: size U.S. 5 (3.75 mm): 24" (60 cm) circular (cir).

Adjust needle size if necessary to obtain the correct gauge.

Notions
Markers (m); cable needle (cn); tapestry needle.

Gauge
Note: All gauges are with one strand each of MC and CC held tog.

16 sts and 25½ rows = 4" (10 cm) in seed st on larger needles.

21½ sts and 25½ rows = 4" (10 cm) in repeated section of Chart A or C on larger needles.

13-st zigzag section of Chart A or C measures 2" (5 cm) wide on larger needles.

44 sts of Chart B measure 7" (18 cm) wide on larger needles.

34 sts of Chart D measure 5½" (14 cm) wide on larger needles.

Worked in pieces from the bottom up and seamed, this standard-fitting cabled pullover features raglan sleeve shaping. A strand each of worsted-weight wool and sportweight metallic yarns are held together throughout for a dense, yet sparkly, take on the classic fisherman's sweater. The cables provide subtle shaping throughout the body.

Hold one strand of each yarn together throughout.

Refer to Chapter 1 for general knitting foundations.

RT: On RS, sl 1 st onto cn and hold in back of work, k1tbl, then k1tbl from cn; on WS, sl 1 st onto cn and hold in back of work, p1tbl, then p1tbl from cn.

LT: On RS, sl 1 st onto cn and hold in front of work, k1tbl, then k1tbl from cn; on WS, sl 1 st onto cn and hold in front of work, p1tbl, then p1tbl from cn.

1/1RPC: Sl 1 st onto cn and hold in back of work, k1, then p1 from cn.

1/1LPC: Sl 1 st onto cn and hold in front of work, p1, then k1 from cn.

1/1RPT: Sl 1 st onto cn and hold in back of work, k1tbl, then p1 from cn.

1/1LPT: Sl 1 st onto cn and hold in front of work, p1, then k1tbl from cn.

2/1RPC: Sl 1 st onto cn and hold in back of work, k2, then p1 from cn.

2/1LPC: Sl 2 sts onto cn and hold in front of work, p1, then k2 from cn.

2/2RC: Sl 2 sts onto cn and hold in back of work, k2, then k2 from cn.

2/2LC: Sl 2 sts onto cn and hold in front of work, k2, then k2 from cn.

2/2RC, k1, p1: Sl 2 sts onto cn and hold in back of work, k2, then k1, p1 from cn.

2/2LC, k1, p1: Sl 2 sts onto cn and hold in front of work, k1, p1, then k2 from cn.

2/2RC, p1, k1: Sl 2 sts onto cn and hold in back of work, k2, then p1, k1 from cn.

2/2LC, p1, k1: Sl 2 sts onto cn and hold in front of work, p1, k1, then k2 from cn.

Wrap 6: K2, p2, k2, sl these 6 sts onto cn, wrap yarn counterclockwise around the base of these 6 sts 4 times, then return these 6 sts to right-hand needle.

Back

With smaller needles and holding one strand each of MC and CC tog, CO 102 (110, 118, 126, 134, 146) sts.

Rib set-up row: (RS) [K1, p1] 2 (4, 6, 4, 6, 5) times, k1, [p2, k2] 2 (2, 2, 4, 4, 6) times, p2, [k1, p1] 4 times, k1, p2, k3, p3, k4, p4, k4, p3, k3, p2 (center sts), k3, p3, k4, p4, k4, p3, k3, p2, k1, [p1, k1] 4 times, p2, [k2, p2] 2 (2, 2, 4, 4, 6) times, k1, [p1, k1] 2 (4, 6, 4, 6, 5) times.

Work sts as they appear (knit the knits, and purl the purls) for 11 more rows, ending with a WS row—12 rib rows total; piece measures 2" (5 cm) from CO.

Change to larger needles.

Chart set-up row: (RS) [P1, k1] 2 (4, 6, 4, 6, 5) times for seed st, place marker (pm), work Row 1 of Chart A (see page 113) over 25 (25, 25, 33, 33, 41) sts, pm, work Row 1 of Chart B (see page 113) over center 44 sts, pm, work Row 1 of Chart C (see page 114) over 25 (25, 25, 33, 33, 41) sts, pm, [k1, p1] 2 (4, 6, 4, 6, 5) times.

Working 4 (8, 12, 8, 12, 10) sts at each end of row in seed st (purl the knits, and knit the purls), work even in patt until piece measures 15" (38 cm) from CO for all sizes, ending with a WS row.

Shape Armholes
Note: *During the following shaping, if there are not enough stitches to work a complete cable crossing, work the stitches as they appear (knit or knit through the back loop) instead.*

BO 5 (6, 5, 5, 5, 7) sts at the beg of the next 2 rows—92 (98, 108, 116, 124, 132) sts rem.

Dec row: (RS) Ssk, RT (see Stitch Guide), work in patt to last 4 sts, LT (see Stitch Guide), k2tog—2 sts dec'd.

Next row: (WS) P1, [p1 through back loop (tbl)] 2 times, work in patt to last 3 sts, [p1tbl] 2 times, p1.

Rep the last 2 rows 18 (21, 22, 26, 26, 30) more times, ending with a WS row—54 (54, 62, 62, 70, 70) sts rem; armholes measure 6¼ (7¼, 7½, 8¾, 8¾, 10)" (16 [18.5, 19, 22, 22, 25.5] cm).

Shape Neck

Row 1: (RS) Ssk, RT, work in patt until there are 15 (15, 17, 17, 19, 19) sts on right-hand needle, join a second ball of yarn, BO center 22 (22, 26, 26, 30, 30) sts, work in patt to last 4 sts, LT, k2tog—15 (15, 17, 17, 19, 19) sts rem at each side.

Row 2: (WS) For first group of sts, p1, [p1tbl] 2 times, work in patt to end; for second group of sts, BO 6 (6, 7, 7, 8, 8) sts at neck edge, work in patt to last 3 sts, p1, [p1tbl] 2 times.

Row 3: For first group of sts, ssk, RT, work in patt to end; for second group of sts, BO 6 (6, 7, 7, 8, 8) sts at neck edge, work in patt to last 4 sts, LT, k2tog—8 (8, 9, 9, 10, 10) sts rem at each side.

Row 4: For first group of sts, p1, [p1tbl] 2 times, work in patt to end; for second group of sts, BO 5 (5, 6, 6, 7, 7) sts at neck edge (1 st on right-hand needle after BO), p1tbl 2 times.

Row 5: For first group of sts, ssk, k1; for second group of sts, BO 5 (5, 6, 6, 7, 7) sts at neck edge, (1 st on right-hand needle after BO), k2tog—2 sts rem at each side for all sizes; armholes measure 7 (8, 8¼, 9½, 9½, 10¾)" (18 [20.5, 21, 24, 24, 27.5] cm).

BO all sts.

Front

CO and work as for back to beg of armhole shaping, ending with a WS row—102 (110, 118, 126, 134, 146) sts; piece measures 15" (38 cm) from CO.

Shape Armholes

BO 5 (6, 5, 5, 5, 7) sts at the beg of the next 2 rows—92 (98, 108, 116, 124, 132) sts rem.

Dec row: (RS) Ssk, RT, work in patt to last 4 sts, LT, k2tog—2 sts dec'd.

Next row: (WS) P1, [p1tbl] 2 times, work in patt to last 3 sts, [p1tbl] 2 times, p1.

Rep the last 2 rows 13 (16, 17, 21, 21, 25) more times, ending with a WS row—64 (64, 72, 72, 80, 80) sts rem; armholes measure 4¾ (5¾, 6, 7¼, 7¼, 8½)" (12 [14.5, 15, 18.5, 18.5, 21.5] cm).

Shape Neck

Row 1: (RS) Ssk, RT, work in patt until there are 24 (24, 26, 26, 29, 29) sts on right-hand needle, join a second ball of yarn, BO center 14 (14, 18, 18, 20, 20) sts, work in patt to last 4 sts, LT, k2tog—24 (24, 26, 26, 29, 29) sts rem at each side.

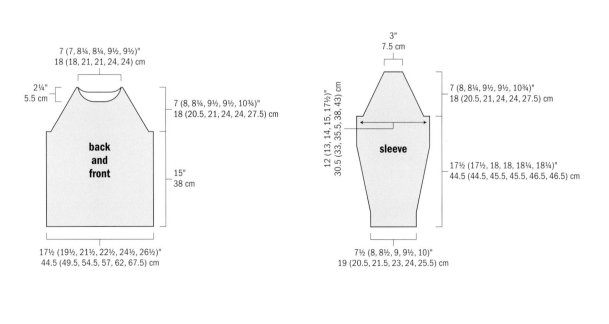

Row 2: (WS) For first group of sts, p1, [p1tbl] 2 times, work in patt to end; for second group of sts, BO 4 (4, 5, 5, 5, 5) sts at neck edge, work in patt to last 3 sts, p1, [p1tbl] 2 times.

Row 3: For first group of sts, ssk, RT, work in patt to end; for second group of sts, BO 4 (4, 5, 5, 5, 5) sts at neck edge, work in patt to last 4 sts, LT, k2tog—19 (19, 20, 20, 23, 23) sts rem at each side.

Row 4: For first group of sts, p1, [p1tbl] 2 times, work in patt to end; for second group of sts, BO 3 (3, 4, 4, 4, 4) sts at neck edge, work in patt to last 3 sts, p1, [p1tbl] 2 times.

Row 5: For first group of sts, ssk, RT, work in patt to end; for second group of sts, BO 3 (3, 4, 4, 4, 4) sts at neck edge, work in patt to last 4 sts, LT, k2tog—15 (15, 15, 15, 18, 18) sts rem at each side.

Maintaining patt as well as possible, dec 1 st at each armhole edge on the next 5 RS rows, and *at the same time* at each neck edge BO 2 (2, 2, 2, 3, 3) sts 3 (3, 3, 3, 2, 2) times, then BO 1 (1, 1, 1, 2, 2) st(s) 2 times, then BO 0 (0, 0, 0, 1, 1) st 0 (0, 0, 0, 1, 1) time—2 sts rem at each side for all sizes; armholes measure 7 (8, 8¼, 9½, 9½, 10¾)" (18 [20.5, 21, 24, 24, 27.5] cm).

BO all sts.

Sleeves

With smaller needles and holding one strand each of MC and CC tog, CO 42 (44, 46, 48, 50, 52) sts.

Rib set-up row: (RS) [K1, p1] 2 (2, 3, 3, 4, 4) times, k3 (4, 3, 4, 3, 4), p2, k3, p3, k4, p4, k4, p3, k3, p2, k3 (4, 3, 4, 3, 4), [p1, k1] 2 (2, 3, 3, 4, 4) times.

Work sts as they appear for 11 more rows, ending with a WS row—12 rib rows total; piece measures 2" (5 cm).

Change to larger needles.

Chart set-up row: (RS) [P1, k1] 2 (2, 3, 3, 4, 4) times for seed st, p 0 (1, 0, 1, 0, 1), pm, work Row 1 of Chart D over center 34 sts, pm, p0 (1, 0, 1, 0, 1), [k1, p1] 2 (2, 3, 3, 4, 4) times.

□	knit on RS; purl on WS
·	purl on RS; knit on WS
Ω	k1tbl on RS; p1tbl on WS
□	pattern repeat
⧅	RT
⧄	LT
⬙	1/1RPC
⬗	1/1LPC
⬙	1/1RPT
⬗	1/1LPT
⬔	2/1RPC
⬓	2/1LPC
⧄	2/2RC
⧅	2/2LC
⬔	2/2RC, k1, p1
⬓	2/2LC, k1, p1
⬔	2/2RC, p1, k1
⬓	2/2LC, p1, k1
⟵·⟶	wrap 6

See Stitch Guide for cable and wrap symbols.

CHART A

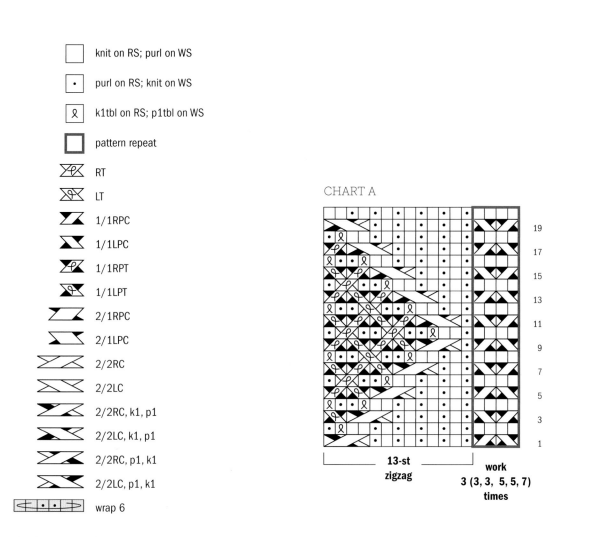

13-st
zigzag

work
3 (3, 3, 5, 5, 7)
times

19
17
15
13
11
9
7
5
3
1

CHART B

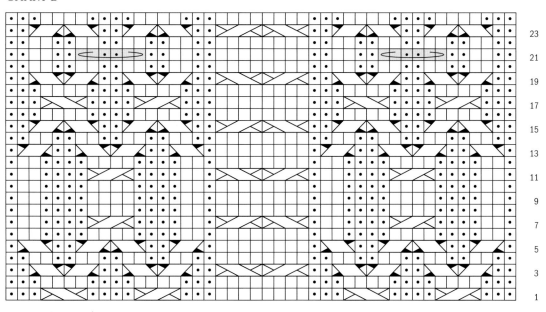

23
21
19
17
15
13
11
9
7
5
3
1

Working 4 (5, 6, 7, 8, 9) sts at each end of row in seed st, work even in patt until piece measures 2½" (6.5 cm) from CO, ending with a WS row.

Inc row: (RS) P1, M1 (see Glossary), work in patt to last st, M1, p1—2 sts inc'd.

Rep inc row every 6th row 0 (0, 0, 0, 0, 10) times, then every 8th row 8 (5, 5, 10, 12, 3) times, then every 10th row 0 (4, 5, 1, 0, 0) times, working new sts into established seed st patt—60 (64, 68, 72, 76, 80) sts.

Work even until piece measures 17½ (17½, 18, 18, 18¼, 18¼)" (44.5 [44.5, 45.5, 45.5, 46.5, 46.5] cm) from CO, ending with a WS row.

CHART C

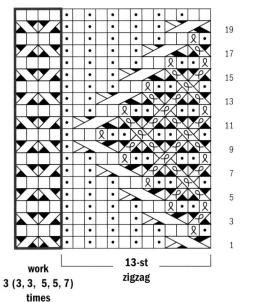

work
**3 (3, 3, 5, 5, 7)
times**

**13-st
zigzag**

19
17
15
13
11
9
7
5
3
1

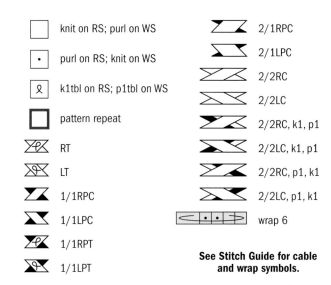

☐ knit on RS; purl on WS	2/1RPC
• purl on RS; knit on WS	2/1LPC
ℓ k1tbl on RS; p1tbl on WS	2/2RC
☐ pattern repeat	2/2LC
RT	2/2RC, k1, p1
LT	2/2LC, k1, p1
1/1RPC	2/2RC, p1, k1
1/1LPC	2/2LC, p1, k1
1/1RPT	wrap 6
1/1LPT	

See Stitch Guide for cable and wrap symbols.

CHART D

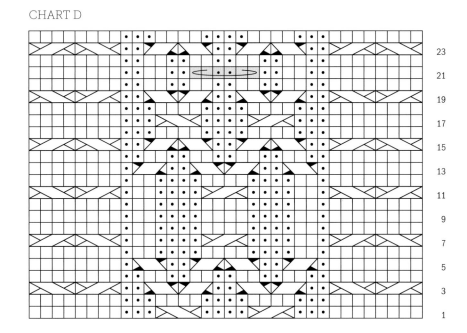

23
21
19
17
15
13
11
9
7
5
3
1

Shape Cap

BO 5 (6, 5, 5, 5, 7) sts at the beg of the next 2 rows—50 (52, 58, 62, 66, 66) sts rem.

Dec row: (RS) Ssk, RT, work in patt to last 4 sts, LT, k2tog—2 sts dec'd.

Next row: (WS) P1, [p1tbl] 2 times, work in patt to last 3 sts, [p1tbl] 2 times, p1.

Next row: K1, [k1tbl] 2 times, work in patt to last 3 sts, [k1tbl] 2 times, k1.

Next row: P1, [p1tbl] 2 times, work in patt to last 3 sts, [p1tbl] 2 times, p1.

Rep the last 4 rows 5 (7, 5, 7, 5, 9) more times—38 (36, 46, 46, 54, 46) sts rem.

[Rep the dec row, then work 1 WS row even] 9 (8, 13, 13, 17, 13) times, then work dec row once more—18 sts rem for all sizes; sleeve cap measures 7 (8, 8¼, 9½, 9½, 10¾)" (18 [20.5, 21, 24, 24, 27.5] cm).

BO all sts.

Finishing

Block pieces to measurements. With just MC threaded on a tapestry needle, sew raglan sleeve caps to raglan armholes. Sew side and sleeve seams.

Neckband

With smaller cir needle, one strand each of MC and CC held tog, and RS facing, pick up and knit 148 (148, 156, 156, 164, 164) sts evenly spaced around neck opening.

Place marker (pm) and join for working in rnds.

Next rnd: *K1, p1; rep from *.

Cont in k1, p1 rib until piece measures 1" (2.5 cm) from pick-up row.

BO all sts in rib patt.

Weave in loose ends.

Catalunya

funnel-neck pullover

An allover bobble pattern gives a pleasingly subtle texture to this standard-fitting pullover. Worked in a metallic yarn, the pullover, with its three-quarter-length set-in sleeves, hemmed edges, and funnel neck, imparts a sense of elegance that can be played up or down.

Finished Size

About 35 (39, 43, 47½, 51½, 55)" (89 [99, 109, 120.5, 131, 139.5] cm) bust circumference.

Designed to be worn with about 3" (7.5 cm) of positive ease.

Pullover shown measures 35" (89 cm).

Yarn

Worsted weight (#4 Medium).

Shown here: Berroco Captiva Metallic (45% cotton, 23% polyester, 19% acrylic, 12% rayon, 1% other; 98 yd [90 m]/50 g): #7507 Polished Iron, 9 (10, 11, 13, 14, 14) skeins.

Needles

Size U.S. 6 (4 mm): 32", 16", and 9" (60, 40, and 20 cm) circular (cir).

Note: *Set of 4 or 5 double-pointed needles (dpn) can be substituted for the 9" (20 cm) cir needle.*

Adjust needle size if necessary to obtain the correct gauge.

Notions

Markers (m); smooth, contrasting waste yarn; size G/6 (4 mm) crochet hook for provisional CO; stitch holders; tapestry needle; strip of heavyweight interfacing measuring 18 (18, 20, 20, 22, 22)" (45.5 [45.5, 51, 51, 56, 56] cm) long and 1" (2.5 cm) wide; sharp-point sewing needle; sewing thread to match yarn color.

Gauge

19 sts and 26 rows/rnds = 4" (10 cm) in St st.

17 sts and 25 rows/rnds = 4" (10 cm) in Reverse Raindrop patts.

notes

The lower body and sleeve lengths shown on the schematic are with the hems finished.

Refer to Chapter 1 for general knitting foundations.

Raindrop: When working in rows, on WS rows knit into the next st in the row below, leaving original st on needle, sl new st onto left needle tip and knit it again, then knit the original st and pass the new st over it.

When working in rnds, purl into the next st in the row below, leaving original st on needle, sl new st onto left needle tip and purl it again, then purl the original st and pass the new st over it.

Reverse Raindrop Pattern in Rows (multiple of 4 sts + 1)

Rows 1 and 3: (RS) Purl.

Row 2: (WS) K1, *work raindrop in next st (see above), k3; rep from *.

Row 4: K3, *work raindrop in next st, k3; rep from * to last 2 sts, work raindrop in next st, k1.

Rep Rows 1–4 for patt.

Reverse Raindrop Pattern in Rounds (multiple of 4 sts)

Rnds 1 and 3: Purl.

Rnd 2: *Work raindrop in next st (see above); p3; rep from *.

Rnd 4: P2, *work raindrop in next st, p3; rep from * to last 2 sts, work raindrop in next st, p1.

Rep Rnds 1–4 for patt.

Hem fold line: (RS) Purl, working each st through the back loop (tbl).

Next row: (WS) Knit and *at the same time* dec 9 (10, 11, 11, 12, 13) sts evenly spaced—74 (83, 91, 101, 109, 117) sts rem.

Next row: (RS) P1 (2, 2, 0, 0, 0), work Row 1 of reverse raindrop in rows patt (see Stitch Guide) to end.

Next row: (WS) Work Row 2 of reverse raindrop patt to last 1 (2, 2, 0, 0, 0) st(s), k1 (2, 2, 0, 0, 0).

Keeping any sts outside reverse raindrop patt in Rev St st (purl on RS, knit on WS), work even until piece measures 14½" (37 cm) from hem fold line, ending with a WS row.

Shape Armholes

BO 4 (4, 4, 6, 6, 6) sts at the beg of the next 2 rows, then BO 2 (2, 3, 3, 4, 4) sts at the beg of the foll 2 (4, 2, 4, 2, 2) rows—62 (67, 77, 77, 89, 97) sts rem.

Sizes 43 (47½, 51½, 55)" (109 [120.5, 131, 139.5] cm) only
BO 2 (2, 3, 3) sts at the beg of the next 4 (2, 4, 4) rows, then BO 0 (0, 2, 2) sts at the beg of the foll 0 (0, 2, 6) rows—69 (73, 73, 73) sts rem.

All sizes
Dec 1 st at each armhole edge every RS row 4 (4, 4, 4, 3, 3) times—54 (59, 61, 65, 67, 67) sts rem.

Work even until armholes measure 7 (7½, 8, 8½, 9, 9½)" (18 [19, 20.5, 21.5, 23, 24] cm), ending with a WS row.

Shape Shoulders

BO 4 (5, 5, 6, 5, 5) sts at beg of next 4 rows—38 (39, 41, 41, 47, 47) sts rem for back neck. Place sts onto holder.

Back

....

With waste yarn, use the crochet provisional method (see Glossary) to CO 83 (93, 102, 112, 121, 130) sts onto 32" (80 cm) cir needle. Do not join.

Change to main yarn. Work in St st for 6 rows, ending with a WS row.

Front

....

CO and work as for back—38 (39, 41, 41, 47, 47) sts rem for front neck. Place sts onto holder.

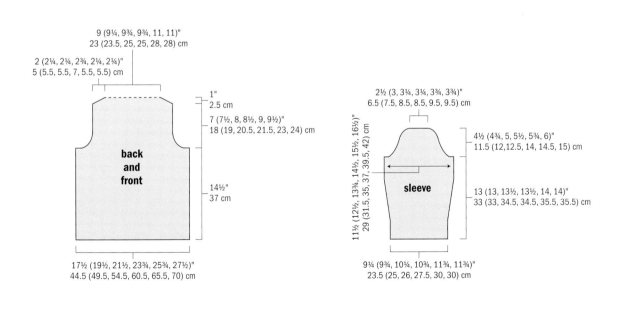

9 (9¼, 9¾, 9¾, 11, 11)"
23 (23.5, 25, 25, 28, 28) cm

2 (2¼, 2¼, 2¾, 2¼, 2¼)"
5 (5.5, 5.5, 7, 5.5, 5.5) cm

1"
2.5 cm

7 (7½, 8, 8½, 9, 9½)"
18 (19, 20.5, 21.5, 23, 24) cm

**back
and
front**

14½"
37 cm

17½ (19½, 21½, 23¾, 25¾, 27½)"
44.5 (49.5, 54.5, 60.5, 65.5, 70) cm

2½ (3, 3¼, 3¼, 3¾, 3¾)"
6.5 (7.5, 8.5, 8.5, 9.5, 9.5) cm

4½ (4¾, 5, 5½, 5¾, 6)"
11.5 (12,12.5, 14, 14.5, 15) cm

sleeve

11½ (12½, 13¾, 14½, 15½, 16½)"
29 (31.5, 35, 37, 39.5, 42) cm

13 (13, 13½, 13½, 14, 14)"
33 (33, 34.5, 34.5, 35.5, 35.5) cm

9¼ (9¾, 10¼, 10¾, 11¾, 11¾)"
23.5 (25, 26, 27.5, 30, 30) cm

Sleeves

With waste yarn, use the crochet provisional method to CO 44 (46, 48, 51, 56, 56) sts onto 32" (80 cm) cir needle. Do not join.

Change to main yarn. Work in St st for 6 rows, ending with a WS row.

Hem fold line: (RS) Purl, working all sts tbl.

Next row: (WS) Knit and *at the same time* dec 5 (5, 4, 5, 6, 6) sts evenly spaced—39 (41, 44, 46, 50, 50) sts rem.

Next row: (RS) P2 (0, 3, 1, 1, 1), work Row 1 of reverse raindrop in rows patt to end.

Next row: (WS) Work Row 2 of reverse raindrop patt to last 2 (0, 3, 1, 1, 1) st(s), k2 (0, 3, 1, 1, 1).

Keeping any sts outside reverse raindrop patt in Rev St st, work even until piece measures 3" (7.5 cm) from hem fold line, ending with a WS row.

Inc row: (RS) P1, M1P (see Glossary), work in patt to last st, M1P, p1—2 sts inc'd.

Rep inc row every 10 (8, 8, 8, 8, 6)th row 4 (5, 6, 3, 4, 9) more times, then every 0 (0, 0, 6, 6, 0)th row 0 (0, 0, 4, 3, 0) more times, incorporating new sts into reverse raindrop patt—49 (53, 58, 62, 66, 70) sts.

Work even until sleeve measures 13 (13, 13½, 13½, 14, 14)" (33 [33, 34.5, 34.5, 35.5, 35.5] cm) from hem fold line, ending with a WS row.

Shape Cap

BO 4 (4, 4, 6, 6, 6) sts at the beg of the next 2 rows—41 (45, 50, 50, 54, 58) sts rem.

BO 2 sts at beg of the next 4 (4, 6, 6, 6, 6) rows, then BO 1 st at the beg of the foll 6 (8, 8, 8, 10, 14) rows—27 (29, 30, 30, 32, 32) sts rem.

[BO 1 st at beg of next 2 rows, then work 2 rows even] 2 (2, 2, 3, 3, 2) times—23 (25, 26, 24, 26, 28) sts rem.

BO 1 st at the beg of the next 4 (4, 4, 2, 2, 4) rows, then BO 2 sts at the beg of the foll 4 rows—11 (13, 14, 14, 16, 16) sts rem. BO all sts.

Finishing

With yarn threaded on a tapestry needle, sew side seams. Sew shoulder seams. Sew sleeve seams. Sew sleeve caps into armholes, matching center of cap BO with shoulder seam and matching sleeve seam with side seam at underarm.

Hems

Carefully remove waste yarn from provisional CO of front and back and place 166 (186, 204, 224, 242, 260) exposed sts onto longest cir needle. Fold hem to WS along fold line. With yarn threaded on a tapestry needle, sew live sts in place on WS, matching the elasticity of the knitted fabric.

Carefully remove waste yarn from provisional CO of sleeve and place 44 (46, 48, 51, 56, 56) exposed sts onto 9" (20 cm) cir needle or dpn. Fold sleeve hem to WS of pullover along fold line, and use yarn threaded on a tapestry needle to sew live sts in place on WS as for lower body.

Block to measurements.

Neckband

With RS facing and 16" (40 cm) cir needle, p38 (39, 41, 41, 47, 47) held back neck sts, pick up and purl (see Glossary) 4 (3, 5, 5, 5, 5) sts between front and back centered on left shoulder seam, p38 (39, 41, 41, 47, 47) held front neck sts, pick up and purl 4 (3, 5, 5, 5, 5) sts between front and back centered on right shoulder seam—84 (84, 92, 92, 104, 104) sts total. Pm and join for working in rnds.

Work in reverse raindrop patt in rounds (see Stitch Guide) for 1¼" (3.2 cm).

Hem fold line: Purl, working all sts tbl.

Work in St st for 6 rnds.

With sharp-point sewing needle and thread, sew short ends of interfacing strip tog.

Fold neck hem to WS along fold line, sandwiching the strip of interfacing between the neckband layers. Use yarn threaded on a tapestry needle to sew live sts in place on WS as for lower body.

Weave in loose ends.

Chapter 5

Outerwear

Before you leave the house, I hope that you reach for one of the three garments I designed for the outerwear chapter. Your jacket shouldn't be an afterthought, but instead an extension of the time and care you've taken to get yourself ready for the day. Knitters usually think of knits as layering pieces, but they are also fantastic for outerwear. I've designed three distinct looks that allow you to leave the house feeling confident and beautiful.

The *Asciano Tweed Moto Jacket* (page 124) is a knitted version of the classic motorcycle jacket—complete with an asymmetrical front and exposed zippers. But this jacket kicks it up a notch by combining worsted-weight wool with a sportweight metallic yarn for an overall look of pure glam. The tight weave of the tweed stitch is impervious to wind and provides a structured fabric that won't sag under the weight of the metal zippers.

The *Shinshiro Herringbone Cape* (page 132) is, in a word, chic. From the classic raglan shape and funnel-neck collar to the allover herringbone stitch motif, Shinshiro is the epitome of femininity. Like many of the designs in this book, it's easy to wear and works equally well with jeans and evening attire.

The *Maestranza Cropped Jacket* (page 138) is ideal for spring and fall. With its bulky bobble stitch, classic Chanel jacket shape, and three-quarter-length sleeves, it's a nice complement to whatever you wear as you walk out the door. The two-color bobble motif is surprising simple to knit—only one color is used per row of knitting. Applied I-cord edging completes the couture appeal of the Maestranza.

Asciano

tweed moto jacket

Finished Size

About 35½ (39½, 43½, 47½, 51½, 55½)" (90 [100.5, 110.5, 120.5, 131, 141] cm) bust circumference.

Designed to be worn with 3½" (9 cm) of positive ease.

Jacket shown measures 35½" (90 cm).

Yarn

Worsted weight (#4 Medium) and Sportweight (#2 Fine).

Shown here: Cascade Yarns Cascade 220 (100% Peruvian highland wool; 220 yd [200 m]/100 g): #2410 Purple (MC), 7 (7, 8, 9, 10, 10) skeins.

Katia Yarns Gatsby (77% viscose, 15% nylon, 8% metallic polyester; 129 yd [118 m]/50 g): #47 Eggplant/Silver (CC), 11 (12, 14, 16, 16, 17) balls.

Needles

Size U.S. 7 (4.5 mm).

Adjust needle size if necessary to obtain the correct gauge.

Notions

Stitch holders; tapestry needle; one 23 (23, 24, 24, 25, 25)" (58.5 [58.5, 61, 61, 63.5, 63.5] cm) separating zipper with metal teeth; two 7" (18 cm) non-separating zippers with metal teeth; sharp-point sewing needle; sewing thread to match yarn color; two size 4 (15 mm) large snaps; one size 000 (7 mm) small snap; two ¾" (2 cm) buttons.

Gauge

20 sts and 38 rows = 4" (10 cm) in tweed st patt with one strand each of MC and CC held tog.

This asymmetrical jacket is knitted in a tweed stitch with a worsted-weight wool held together with a slightly glitzy novelty yarn. The pieces are knitted from the bottom up and seamed together. The result is thick and windproof but ultra stylish, with zippers along the asymmetrical front opening and sleeve cuffs.

notes

Hold one strand each of MC and CC together throughout.

Refer to Chapter 1 for general knitting foundations.

Tweed Stitch (odd number of sts)

Row 1: (RS) K1, *sl 1 pwise with yarn in front (wyf), k1; rep from *.

Row 2: (WS) P2, *sl 1 pwise with yarn in back (wyb), p1; rep from * to last st, p1.

Rep Rows 1 and 2 for patt.

Reverse Tweed Stitch (odd number of sts)

Row 1: (RS) P2, *sl 1 pwise with yarn in back (wyb), p1; rep from * to last st, p1.

Row 2: (WS) K1, *sl 1 pwise with yarn in front (wyf), k1; rep from *.

Rep Rows 1 and 2 for patt.

Back

Holding one strand each of MC and CC tog, CO 89 (99, 109, 119, 129, 139) sts. Work in reverse tweed st patt (see Stitch Guide) until piece measures 2" (5 cm) from CO, ending with a WS row. Change to tweed st patt (see Stitch Guide) and work even until piece measures 15" (38 cm) from CO for all sizes, ending with a WS row.

Shape Armholes

Keeping in patt, BO 5 (5, 5, 8, 8, 8) sts at the beg of the next 2 rows, then BO 2 (3, 3, 4, 4, 4) sts at the beg of the foll 2 (2, 4, 2, 2, 2) rows—75 (83, 87, 95, 105, 115) sts rem.

BO 1 (2, 2, 2, 3, 3) st(s) at the beg of the next 6 (2, 2, 4, 2, 4) rows, then BO 0 (1, 1, 1, 2, 2) st(s) at the beg of the foll 0 (4, 4, 2, 4, 2) rows, then BO 0 (0, 0, 0, 1, 1) st at the beg of the foll 0 (0, 0, 0, 2, 4) rows—69 (75, 79, 85, 89, 95) sts rem.

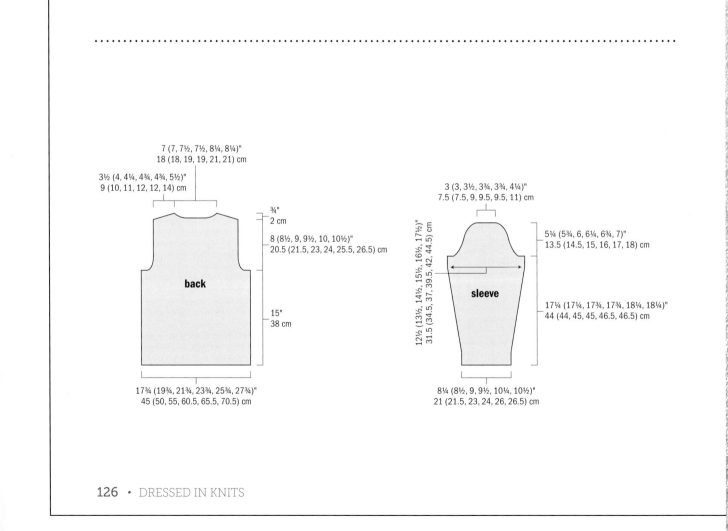

7 (7, 7½, 7½, 8¼, 8¼)"
18 (18, 19, 19, 21, 21) cm

3½ (4, 4¼, 4¾, 4¾, 5½)"
9 (10, 11, 12, 12, 14) cm

¾"
2 cm

8 (8½, 9, 9½, 10, 10½)"
20.5 (21.5, 23, 24, 25.5, 26.5) cm

back

15"
38 cm

17¾ (19¾, 21¾, 23¾, 25¾, 27¾)"
45 (50, 55, 60.5, 65.5, 70.5) cm

3 (3, 3½, 3¾, 3¾, 4¼)"
7.5 (7.5, 9, 9.5, 9.5, 11) cm

5¼ (5¾, 6, 6¼, 6¾, 7)"
13.5 (14.5, 15, 16, 17, 18) cm

12½ (13½, 14½, 15½, 16½, 17½)"
31.5 (34.5, 37, 39.5, 42, 44.5) cm

sleeve

17¼ (17¼, 17¾, 17¾, 18¼, 18¼)"
44 (44, 45, 45, 46.5, 46.5) cm

8¼ (8½, 9, 9½, 10¼, 10½)"
21 (21.5, 23, 24, 26, 26.5) cm

Work even until armholes measure 8 (8½, 9, 9½, 10, 10½)" (20.5 [21.5, 23, 24, 25.5, 26.5] cm), ending with a WS row.

Shape Neck and Shoulders

Keeping in patt, BO 5 (5, 6, 6, 6, 7) sts at the beg of the next 2 rows—59 (65, 67, 73, 77, 81) sts rem.

Next row: (RS) BO 4 (5, 5, 6, 6, 7) sts, work in patt until there are 17 (19, 19, 21, 22, 23) sts on right needle, join new yarn and BO 17 (17, 19, 19, 21, 21) center sts, work in patt to end—17 (19, 19, 21, 22, 23) sts rem for right shoulder and 21 (24, 24, 27, 28, 30) sts rem for left shoulder.

Place right shoulder sts onto holder.

Left Shoulder

Next row: (WS) Keeping in patt, BO 4 (5, 5, 6, 6, 7) sts, work to end—17 (19, 19, 21, 22, 23) sts rem.

Next row: (RS) BO 5 sts at neck edge, work in patt to end—12 (14, 14, 16, 17, 18) sts rem.

Next row: BO 4 (5, 5, 6, 6, 7) sts, work in patt to end—8 (9, 9, 10, 11, 11) sts rem.

Next row: BO 4 (4, 4, 4, 5, 5) sts at neck edge, work in patt to end—4 (5, 5, 6, 6, 6) sts rem.

BO all sts.

Right Shoulder

With WS facing, return 17 (19, 19, 21, 22, 23) held right shoulder sts onto needle and rejoin yarn.

Next row: (WS) Keeping in patt, BO 5 sts at neck edge, work in patt to end—12 (14, 14, 16, 17, 18) sts rem.

Next row: (RS) BO 4 (5, 5, 6, 6, 7) sts, work in patt to end—8 (9, 9, 10, 11, 11) sts rem.

Next row: BO 4 (4, 4, 4, 5, 5) sts at neck edge, work in patt to end—4 (5, 5, 6, 6, 6) sts rem.

BO all sts.

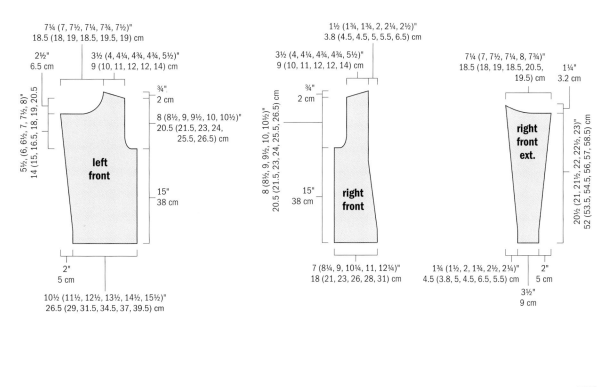

Left Front

Holding one strand each of MC and CC tog, CO 53 (57, 63, 67, 73, 77) sts. Work in reverse tweed st patt until piece measures 2" (5 cm) from CO, ending with a WS row.

Shape Front Edge and Armhole

Note: *Armhole shaping begins while front edge shaping is in progress; read all the way through the following section before proceeding.*

Change to tweed st.

Inc row: (RS) Work in tweed st to last st, M1 (see Glossary), k1—1 st inc'd at front edge.

Keeping in patt, rep inc row every 18 (20, 20, 20, 20, 20)th row 3 (9, 9, 6, 4, 1) more time(s), then every 20th (0, 0, 22nd, 22nd, 22nd) row 6 (0, 0, 3, 5, 8) times, incorporating new sts into tweed st patt—10 sts total added at front edge for all sizes.

At the same time, when piece measures 15" (38 cm) from CO, at armhole edge (beg of RS rows) BO 5 (5, 5, 8, 8, 8) sts once, then BO 2 (3, 3, 4, 4, 4) sts 1 (1, 2, 1, 1, 1) time(s), then BO 1 (2, 2, 2, 3, 3) st(s) 3 (1, 1, 2, 1, 2) time(s), then BO 0 (1, 1, 1, 2, 2) st(s) 0 (2, 2, 1, 2, 1) time(s), then BO 0 (0, 0, 0, 1, 1) st(s) 0 (0, 0, 0, 1, 2) time(s)—10 (12, 15, 17, 20, 22) sts total removed from armhole edge; 53 (55, 58, 60, 63, 65) sts rem when all front and armhole shaping is complete.

Work even in patt until armhole measures 5½ (6, 6½, 7, 7½, 8)" (14 [15, 16.5, 18, 19, 20.5] cm), ending with a RS row.

Shape Neck

Keeping in patt, at neck edge (beg of WS rows), BO 19 (18, 18, 17, 19, 18) sts once, then BO 9 (9, 9, 9, 10, 10) sts once, then BO 4 sts once, then BO 2 (2, 3, 3, 3, 3) sts once, then BO 1 (1, 2, 2, 2, 2) st(s) 2 (2, 1, 1, 1, 1) time(s), then BO 0 (0, 1, 1, 1, 1) st(s) 0 (0, 1, 1, 1, 1) time—17 (20, 21, 24, 24, 27) sts rem.

Work even until armhole measures 8 (8½, 9, 9½, 10, 10½)" (20.5 [21.5, 23, 24, 25.5, 26.5] cm), ending with a WS row.

Shape Shoulder

At armhole edge (beg of RS rows), BO 5 (5, 6, 6, 6, 7) sts once, then BO 4 (5, 5, 6, 6, 7) sts 2 times, then BO 4 (5, 5, 6, 6, 6) sts once—no sts rem.

Right Front

Holding one strand each of MC and CC tog, CO 35 (41, 45, 51, 55, 61) sts. Work in reverse tweed st patt until piece measures 2" (5 cm) from CO, ending with a WS row.

Shape Inner Edge

Note: *The inner edge (beg of RS rows; end of WS rows) is the selvedge that will be sewn to the right front extension.*

Change to tweed st.

Dec row: (RS) Ssk, work in patt to end—1 st dec'd at front edge.

Keeping in patt, rep dec row every 14th (14th, 12th, 12th, 10th, 10th) row 7 (1, 8, 3, 10, 6) more time(s), then every 0 (12th, 0, 10th, 0, 8th) row 0 (7, 0, 6, 0, 5) times—27 (32, 36, 41, 44, 49) sts rem.

Work even until piece measures 15" (38 cm) from CO for all sizes, ending with a RS row.

Shape Armhole

Keeping in patt, at armhole edge (beg of WS rows) BO 5 (5, 5, 8, 8, 8) sts once, then BO 2 (3, 3, 4, 4, 4) sts 1 (1, 2, 1, 1, 1) time(s), then BO 1 (2, 2, 2, 3, 3) st(s) 3 (1, 1, 2, 1, 2) time(s), then BO 0 (1, 1, 1, 2, 2) st(s) 0 (2, 2, 1, 2, 1) time(s), then BO 0 (0, 0, 0, 1, 1) st 0 (0, 0, 0, 1, 2) time(s)—17 (20, 21, 24, 24, 27) sts rem.

Work even until piece measures 8 (8½, 9, 9½, 10, 10½)" (20.5 [21.5, 23, 24, 25.5, 26.5] cm) from CO, ending with a RS row.

Shape Shoulder

At armhole edge (beg of WS rows), BO 5 (5, 6, 6, 6, 7) sts once, then BO 4 (5, 5, 6, 6, 7) sts 2 times, then BO 4 (5, 5, 6, 6, 6) sts once—no sts rem.

Right Front Extension

Holding one strand of MC and CC tog, CO 17 sts.

Work in reverse tweed st patt until piece measures 2" (5 cm) from CO, ending with a RS row.

Shape Edges

Note: *Edge shaping occurs simultaneously along the inner edge (beg of WS rows), which will be sewn to the right front, and along the front edge (beg of RS rows); read all the way through the following section before proceeding.*

Change to tweed st.

Inner edge inc row: (WS) K1, M1, work in patt to end—1 st inc'd at inner edge.

Keeping in patt, inc 1 st at the inner edge every 20th (24th, 20th, 22nd, 16th, 18th) row 8 (7, 9, 8, 11, 10) more times, incorporating new sts into tweed st patt—9 (8, 10, 9, 12, 11) sts total added at beg of WS rows.

At the same time, beg on the first RS row after the inner edge inc row, shape front edge as foll.

Front edge inc row: (RS) K1, M1, work in patt to end—1 st inc'd at front edge.

Keeping in patt, inc 1 st at the front edge every 18th (18th, 18th, 20th, 20th, 20th) row 6 (5, 4, 9, 6, 4) more times, then every 20th (20th, 20th, 0, 22nd, 22nd) row 3 (4, 5, 0, 3, 5) times, incorporating new sts into tweed st patt—10 sts total added at beg of RS rows; 36 (35, 37, 36, 39, 38) sts when all shaping is complete.

Work even until piece measures 20½ (21, 21½, 22,

22½, 23)" (52 [53.5, 54.5, 56, 57, 58.5] cm) from CO, ending with a RS row.

Shape Neck

Keeping in patt, at neck edge (beg of RS rows), BO 19 (18, 18, 17, 19, 18) sts once, then BO 9 (9, 9, 9, 10, 10) sts once, then BO 4 sts once, then BO 2 (2, 3, 3, 3, 3) sts once, then BO 1 (1, 2, 2, 2, 2) st(s) 2 (2, 1, 1, 1, 1) time(s), then BO 0 (0, 1, 1, 1, 1) st 0 (0, 1, 1, 1, 1) time—no sts rem.

Sleeves

· ·

Note: *Sleeves are worked entirely in tweed stitch.*

Holding one strand each of MC and CC tog, CO 41 (43, 45, 47, 51, 53) sts. Work in tweed st until piece measures 2" (5 cm) from CO for all sizes, ending with a WS row.

Inc row: (RS) K1, M1, work in patt to last st, M1, k1—2 sts inc'd.

Keeping in patt, rep inc row every 12th (12th, 10th, 10th, 8th, 8th) row 6 (11, 9, 14, 2, 7) more times, then every 14th (0, 12th, 0, 10th, 10th) row 4 (0, 4, 0, 13, 9) times, incorporating new sts into tweed st patt—63 (67, 73, 77, 83, 87) sts.

Work even until piece measures 17¼ (17¼, 17¾, 17¾, 18¼, 18¼)" (44 [44, 45, 45, 46.5, 46.5] cm) from CO, ending with a WS row.

Shape Cap

Keeping in patt, BO 5 (5, 5, 8, 8, 8) sts at the beg of the next 2 rows—53 (57, 63, 61, 67, 71) sts rem.

Dec row: (RS) Ssk, work in patt to last 2 sts, k2tog—2 sts dec'd.

Keeping in patt, rep dec row every 4th row 9 (9, 8, 11, 10, 11) times, then every RS row 4 (6, 9, 4, 8, 8) times—25 (25, 27, 29, 29, 31) sts rem.

BO 3 sts at the beg of the next 2 rows, then BO 2 sts at the beg of the foll 2 rows—15 (15, 17, 19, 19, 21) sts rem.

BO all sts.

Finishing

Block pieces to measurements.

Front Zipper

Separate long zipper in preparation for sewing between right front sections.

Following the instructions on page 19 and using sharp-point sewing needle and thread, sew the half of the zipper without the zipper pull to WS of right front inner edge, with bottom of zipper aligned with lower edge of body. Sew the half with the zipper pull to the WS of the left front edge, aligning the bottom of the zipper with the lower edge of body.

With MC threaded on a tapestry needle, sew inner edges of right front and right front extension together so that the zipper teeth are on the RS of the garment, on top of the extension.

Collar

With MC threaded on a tapestry needle, sew shoulder seams. With RS facing and beg 4 (3¾, 3¾, 3½, 4, 3¾)" (10 [9.5, 9.5, 9, 10, 9.5] cm) from right front edge, pick up and knit 107 (107, 111, 111, 115, 115) sts evenly spaced along neckline, ending 4 (3¾, 3¾, 3½, 4, 3¾)" (10 [9.5, 9.5, 9, 10, 9.5] cm) from left front edge.

Next row: (WS) Work Row 2 of tweed st to end, then use the backward-loop method (see Glossary) to CO 16 (16, 18, 18, 20, 20) sts for button tab—123 (123, 129, 129, 135, 135) sts total.

Next row: (RS) Knit across 16 (16, 18, 18, 20, 20) new sts, work in established tweed st to end.

Change to working all sts in tweed st, and work even until piece measures 2½" (6.5 cm) from pick-up row, ending with a WS row.

With RS facing, BO all sts.

Sleeve Zippers

With MC threaded on a tapestry needle, sew sleeve seam from underarm to 7" (18 cm) above CO edge—seam measures about 10¼ (10¼, 10¾, 10¾, 11¼, 11¼)" (26 [26, 27.5, 27.5, 28.5, 28.5] cm). With sharp-point sewing needle and thread, sew zipper to WS of 7" (18 cm) opening in sleeve seam, with zipper pull at the CO edge.

With MC threaded on a tapestry needle, sew side seams. Sew sleeve caps into armholes, matching center of cap BO with shoulder seam and matching sleeve seam with side seam at underarm.

Weave in loose ends.

Snaps and Buttons

With sharp-point sewing needle and thread, sew two large male snaps to WS of button tab at right front end of collar, each ¾" (2 cm) from a corner of the tab.

Sew two large female snaps to RS of left front collar, each 1" (2.5 cm) in from collar selvedge and ¾" (2 cm) down from the top edge or up from the bottom edge.

Sew two buttons to RS of button tab, each ¾" (2 cm) from a corner and centered on top of large snaps.

Sew small male snap to RS of right front extension at lower corner. Zip the jacket, and sew small female snap to WS of left front, aligned with the position of male snap.

Shinshiro

herringbone cape

Finished Size
About 92 (95½, 99)" (233.5 [242.5, 251.5] cm) circumference at lower edge.

Cape shown measures 92" (233.5 cm) at lower edge.

Yarn
Worsted weight (#4 Medium).

Shown here: Berroco Elements (51% wool, 49% nylon; 153 yd [141m]/50 g): #4905 Nickel, 15 (16, 17) balls.

Needles
Size U.S. 10½ (6.5 mm): 24" (60 cm) or longer circular (cir).

Adjust needle size if necessary to obtain the correct gauge.

Notions
Stitch holder; tapestry needle; piece of fabric measuring 17½" by 15½" (44.5 by 39.5 cm) for pockets; sharp-point sewing needle; sewing thread to match yarn and pocket fabric; two 7" (18 cm) non-separating zippers.

Gauge
26 sts and 18 rows = 4" (10 cm) in herringbone patt.

Worked in a lofty herringbone pattern, this A-line cape is knitted in four pieces that are seamed together for a raglan fit across the shoulders. Special features include zippered pockets and a high funnel-neck opening for a wrap that's both warm and practical.

Measure lengths straight up in the center of the fabric; do not measure along diagonal shaped edges.

The dashed lines on the back and front schematic indicate the location of the pocket openings on the front only.

Refer to Chapter 1 for general knitting foundations.

Herringbone Pattern

Row 1: (RS) K2tog through back loops (tbl), dropping only the first st off left needle tip, *work k2togtbl into rem st and next st after it, dropping only the first st off left needle tip; rep from * to last patt st, k1tbl.

Row 2: (WS) P2tog, dropping only the first st off left needle tip, *work p2tog into rem st and next st after it, dropping only the first st off left needle tip; rep from * to last patt st, p1.

Rep Rows 1 and 2 for patt.

Back

Using the German twisted method (see Glossary), CO 178 (184, 190) sts.

Set-up row: (RS) K1, work Row 1 of herringbone patt (see Stitch Guide) to last st, k1.

Next row: (WS) K1, work Row 2 of herringbone patt to last st, k1.

Work shaping as foll.

Dec row: (RS) K1, ssk, work in established herringbone patt to last 3 sts, k2tog, k1—2 sts dec'd.

Keeping 1 st at each side in garter st (knit every row), [work 3 rows even, then rep the dec row] 4 (2, 1) time(s)—168 (178, 186) sts rem.

[Work 1 row even, then rep the dec row] 60 (64, 66) times—48 (50, 54) sts rem.

Work 1 WS row even—piece measures 31" (79 cm) from CO.

Shape Neck

Next row: (RS) K1, ssk, work in herringbone patt until there are 12 (12, 13) sts on right needle, join new yarn and BO center 22 (24, 26) sts, work in herringbone patt to last 3 sts, k2tog, k1—12 (12, 13) sts rem each side.

Working each side separately, cont to dec 1 st at each side on the next 2 RS rows as established and *at the same time* at each neck edge BO 5 (5, 6) sts once, then BO 5 sts once—no sts rem; piece measures 32" (81.5 cm) from CO.

Front

Work as for back until the dec row has been worked every RS row 19 (23, 25) times—130 (132, 136) sts rem.

Work 1 WS row even—piece measures 13" (33 cm) from CO.

Pocket Openings

Left Front

Next row: (RS) K1, ssk, work 18 sts in herringbone patt, M1 (see Glossary), k1—22 left front sts on right needle. Place rem 108 (110, 114) front sts onto holder.

Work 22 sts as foll.

Next row: (WS) K1, work in herringbone patt to last st, k1.

Next row: (RS) K1, ssk, work in herringbone patt to last st, M1, k1—no change to st count.

Rep the last 2 rows 12 more times, then work the WS row once more—28 rows in pocket opening; piece measures 19¼" (49 cm) from CO. Place 22 left front sts onto holder.

Center Front

With RS facing, place 86 (88, 92) held center sts onto needle, leaving rem 22 right front sts onto holder, and rejoin yarn.

Next row: (RS) K1, ssk, work in herringbone patt to last 3 sts, k2tog, k1—2 sts dec'd.

Next row: (WS) K1, work in herringbone patt to last st, k1.

Rep these 2 rows 13 more times—58 (60, 64) sts rem; 28 rows in pocket opening; piece measures 19¼" (49 cm) from CO. Cut yarn, leaving a 6" (15 cm) tail.

Place 58 (60, 64) center sts onto holder.

Right Front
With RS facing, return 22 held right-front sts onto needle and rejoin yarn.

Next row: (RS) K1, M1, work in herringbone patt to last 3 sts, k2tog, k1—no change to st count.

Next row: (WS) K1, work in herringbone patt to last st, k1.

Rep these 2 rows 13 more times—28 rows in pocket opening; piece measures 19¼" (49 cm) from CO. Leave sts on needle. Cut yarn, leaving a 6" (15 cm) tail.

Join Tops of Pocket Openings
With RS facing, return 58 (60, 64) held center sts to needle, followed by 22 held left-front sts, being careful not to twist pieces, and rejoin yarn—102 (104, 108) sts total.

Resume working across all sts as foll.

Dec row: (RS) K1, ssk, work in herringbone patt to last 3 sts, k2tog, k1—2 sts dec'd.

Keeping 1 st at each side in garter st, [work 1 row even, then rep the dec row] 21 times—58 (60, 64) sts rem.

Work 1 WS row even—piece measures 29" (73.5 cm) from CO.

Shape Neck
Next row: (RS) K1, ssk, work in herringbone patt until there are 21 (22, 22) sts on right needle, join new yarn and BO center 14 (14, 18) sts, work in herringbone patt to last 3 sts, k2tog, k1—21 (22, 22) sts rem each side.

Working each side separately, cont to dec 1 st at each side on the next 7 RS rows as established and *at the same time* at each neck edge BO 4 sts once, then BO 3 (4, 4) sts once, then BO 3 sts once, then BO 2 sts once, then BO 1 st 2 times—no sts rem; piece measures 32" (81.5 cm) from CO.

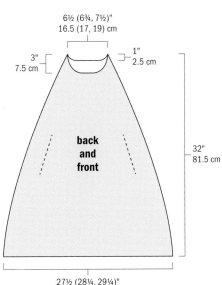

6½ (6¾, 7½)"
16.5 (17, 19) cm

3"
7.5 cm

1"
2.5 cm

back and front

32"
81.5 cm

27½ (28¼, 29¼)"
70 (72, 74.5) cm

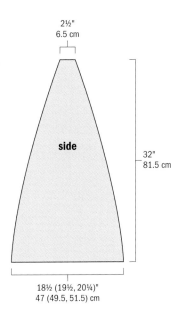

2½"
6.5 cm

side

32"
81.5 cm

18½ (19½, 20¼)"
47 (49.5, 51.5) cm

Sides (Make 2)

Using the German twisted method, CO 120 (126, 132) sts.

Set-up row: (RS) K1, work Row 1 of herringbone patt to last st, k1.

Next row: (WS) K1, work Row 2 of herringbone patt to last st, k1.

Work shaping as foll.

Dec row: (RS) K1, ssk, work in established herringbone patt to last 3 sts, k2tog, k1—2 sts dec'd.

Keeping 1 st at each side in garter st, [work 3 rows even, then rep the dec row] 19 (16, 13) times—80 (92, 104) sts.

[Work 1 row even, then rep the dec row] 32 (38, 44) times—16 sts rem for all sizes.

Work 1 WS row even—piece measures 32" (81.5 cm) from CO. BO all sts.

Finishing

Block pieces to measurements.

With yarn threaded on a tapestry needle, sew back to both side pieces along its entire length. Sew front to side pieces, leaving the bottom 17½" (44.5 cm) unsewn for front slits.

Collar

Notes: *Pick up sts in the row below the BO edge to create a cleaner edge. More stitches are picked up than needed to avoid gaps along the pick-up row; the extra stitches are decreased on the following row.*

Make a slipknot and place on right needle tip. With RS facing and beg at left back seam, pick up and knit 134 (140, 146) sts evenly spaced across top of left side, front, right side, and back, then use the backward-loop method (see Glossary) to CO 1 more st—136 (142, 148) sts total, counting slipknot as 1 st.

Next row: (WS) Purl and *at the same time* dec 30 sts evenly spaced—106 (112, 118) sts rem.

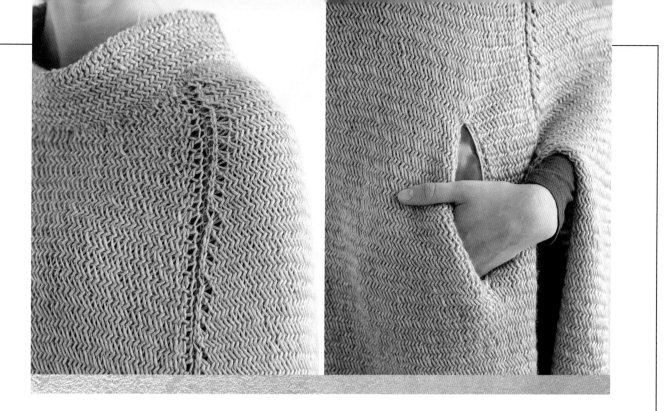

Work in herringbone patt until collar measures 3" (7.5 cm) from pick-up row, ending with a WS row.

Fold line: (RS) *P1tbl; rep from *.

Beg and ending with a WS row, work in herringbone patt, until collar measures 3" (7.5 cm) from fold line and 6" (15 cm) from pick-up row, ending with a WS row.

BO all sts.

With yarn threaded on a tapestry needle, sew selvedges of collar tog. Fold collar in half to WS along fold line and sew BO edge of collar to WS of pick-up row.

Weave in loose ends, using 6" (15 cm) tails at top of each pocket to reinforce the openings.

Zippers

With WS facing, pin each closed zipper to one pocket opening, with the zipper pull at the top of the pocket opening and the teeth visible on the outside of the cape. Take care not to stretch the knitted fabric, and allow any extra zipper length to extend beyond the bottom of the pocket opening on the WS. With sharp-point sewing needle and thread to match yarn, sew zippers in place according to the instructions on page 19.

Pockets

Cut pocket fabric into four equal quarters, each measuring 8¾" (22 cm) wide and 7¾" (19.5 cm) high. Hold two [for consistency] pieces with right sides tog and wrong sides facing out and use sharp-point sewing needle and pocket-colored thread to sew them together around three sides with a ⅝" (1.5 cm) seam, leaving one 8¾" (22 cm) side open.

With wrong sides of pocket still facing out, pin open side of one pocket to the zipper tape. With pocket-colored thread, use backstitches (see Glossary) to sew pocket in place, being careful not to catch yarn when attaching pockets; right side of pocket fabric will be revealed on outside of garment when pocket is unzipped. Repeat for second pocket.

Maestranza

cropped jacket

Finished Size

About 37 (43¼, 46¼, 49½, 56, 59¼)" (94 [110, 117.5, 125.5, 142, 150.5] cm) bust circumference, with 1" (2.5 cm) front edgings meeting at center front (see Notes).

Designed to be worn with about 5" (12.5 cm) of positive ease at the bust.

Jacket shown measures 37" (94 cm).

Yarn

Bulky weight (#5 Bulky).

Shown here: Rowan Big Wool (100% wool; 87 yd [80 m]/100 g): #26 Blue Velvet (MC; navy), 5 (6, 7, 7, 8, 9) balls; #70 Deer (CC; pale sage), 5 (6, 7, 7, 8, 9) balls.

Needles

Size U.S. 13 (9 mm): straight or 24" (60 cm) circular (cir) and set of 2 double-pointed (dpn).

Adjust needle size if necessary to obtain the correct gauge.

Notions

Markers (m); tapestry needle.

Gauge

10 sts and 12 rows = 4" (10 cm) in bobble patt.

This loose-fitting jacket is a fun take on the classic Chanel shape. An allover bobble pattern, worked in stripes of just one color per row, adds textural interest to the couture fit. I-cord edging around the neck and front opening give a polished finish that reflects the I-cord cast-ons along the lower edges of the body and sleeves.

notes

The measurements on the schematic include the slevedge stitches for blocking purposes; the selvedge stitches used in the side seams and to join the front bands are not included in the finished bust measurements.

Refer to Chapter 1 for general knitting foundations.

Bobble: Knit into the front, back, and front of the same st—3 sts made from 1 st. [Turn work, p3, turn work, k3] 2 times, then pass the 2nd and 3rd sts on right needle over the first st and off the needle—3 sts reduced to 1 st again.

Bobble Pattern (multiple of 4 sts + 1)

Note: Change color at the start of each WS row.

Row 1: (RS) With MC, k1, *work bobble (see above) in next st, k3; rep from *.

Row 2: (WS) With CC, purl.

Row 3: With CC, *k3, work bobble in next st; rep from * to last st, k1.

Row 4: With MC, purl.

Rep Rows 1–4 for patt.

Back

With MC and using the I-cord method (see Bukhara Cardigan on page 50), CO 47 (55, 59, 63, 71, 75) sts. Cut yarn, leaving a 6" (15 cm) tail.

Slide CO sts to other needle tip so the first st CO will be the first st worked.

Next row: (RS) With MC, k1 (selvedge st; knit every row), place marker (pm), work Row 1 of bobble patt (see Stitch Guide) over center 45 (53, 57, 61, 69, 73) sts, pm, k1 (selvedge st; knit every row).

Keeping 1 st at each side in garter st, work even in patt until piece measures about 10" (25.5 cm) from CO, ending with WS Row 4 of patt.

Shape Armholes

Keeping in patt, BO 3 (4, 4, 4, 5, 5) sts at the beg of the next 2 rows, then BO 1 (2, 2, 2, 3, 3) st(s) at the beg of the foll 4 (2, 2, 4, 2, 2) rows—37 (43, 47, 47, 55, 59) sts rem.

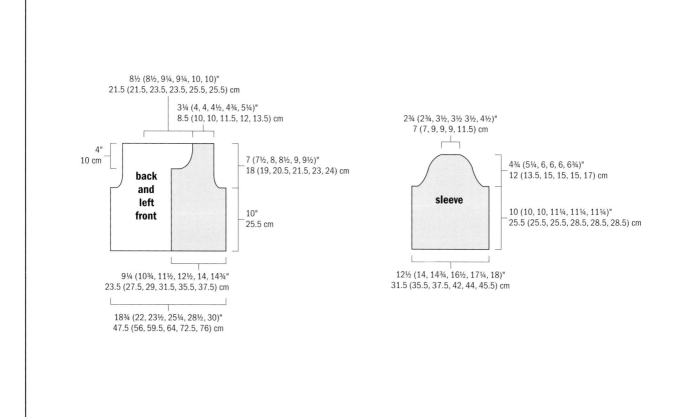

8½ (8½, 9¼, 9¼, 10, 10)"
21.5 (21.5, 23.5, 23.5, 25.5, 25.5) cm

3¼ (4, 4, 4½, 4¾, 5¼)"
8.5 (10, 10, 11.5, 12, 13.5) cm

4"
10 cm

back and left front

7 (7½, 8, 8½, 9, 9½)"
18 (19, 20.5, 21.5, 23, 24) cm

10"
25.5 cm

9¼ (10¾, 11½, 12½, 14, 14¾"
23.5 (27.5, 29, 31.5, 35.5, 37.5) cm

18¾ (22, 23½, 25¼, 28½, 30)"
47.5 (56, 59.5, 64, 72.5, 76) cm

2¾ (2¾, 3½, 3½ 3½, 4½)"
7 (7, 9, 9, 9, 11.5) cm

4¾ (5¼, 6, 6, 6, 6¾)"
12 (13.5, 15, 15, 15, 17) cm

sleeve

10 (10, 10, 11¼, 11¼, 11¼)"
25.5 (25.5, 25.5, 28.5, 28.5, 28.5) cm

12½ (14, 14¾, 16½, 17¼, 18)"
31.5 (35.5, 37.5, 42, 44, 45.5) cm

BO 0 (1, 1, 1, 2, 2) st(s) at the beg of the next 0 (2, 4, 2, 2, 2) rows, then BO 0 (0, 0, 0, 1, 1) st (s) at the beg of the foll 0 (0, 0, 0, 2, 4) rows—37 (41, 43, 45, 49, 51) sts rem.

Re-establish selvedge sts and cont in patt until armholes measure 7 (7½, 8, 8½, 9, 9½)" (18 [19, 20.5, 21.5, 23, 24] cm), ending with a WS row.

BO all sts.

Left Front

With MC and using the I-cord method, CO 23 (27, 29, 31, 35, 37) sts. Cut yarn, leaving a 6" (15 cm) tail.

Slide CO sts to other needle tip so the first st CO will be the first st worked.

Next row: (RS) With MC, k1 (selvedge st; knit every row), k0 (0, 1, 0, 0, 1), pm, work Row 1 of bobble patt over center 21 (25, 25, 29, 33, 33) sts, pm, k0 (0, 1, 0, 0, 1), k1 (selvedge st; knit every row).

Keeping 1 edge st at each side in garter st and working any sts between selvedge sts and marked patt section in St st, work even until piece measures about 10" (25.5 cm) from CO, ending with WS Row 4 of patt.

Shape Armhole
Keeping in patt, at armhole edge (beg of RS rows), BO 3 (4, 4, 4, 5, 5) sts at the beg of the next RS row, then BO 1 (2, 2, 2, 3, 3) st(s) at the beg of the foll 2 (1, 1, 2, 1, 1) RS row(s)—18 (21, 23, 23, 27, 29) sts rem.

BO 0 (1, 1, 1, 2, 2) st(s) at the beg of the next 0 (1, 2, 1, 1, 1) RS row(s), then BO 0 (0, 0, 0, 1, 1) st(s) at the beg of the foll 0 (0, 0, 0, 1, 2) RS row(s)—18 (20, 21, 22, 24, 25) sts rem.

Re-establish selvedge st at armhole edge and cont in patt until armhole measures 3 (3½, 4, 4½, 5, 5½)" (7.5 [9, 10, 11.5, 12.5, 14] cm), ending with a RS row.

Shape Neck

Keeping in patt, at neck edge (beg of WS rows), BO 4 sts once, then BO 2 (2, 3, 3, 3, 3) sts 2 (2, 1, 1, 1, 1) time(s), then BO 1 (1, 2, 2, 2, 2) st(s) 2 (2, 1, 1, 2, 2) time(s), then BO 0 (0, 1, 1, 1, 1) st 0 (0, 2, 2, 1, 1) time(s)—8 (10, 10, 11, 12, 13) sts rem.

Re-establish selvedge st at neck edge and cont in patt until armhole measures 7 (7½, 8, 8½, 9, 9½)" (18 [19, 20.5, 21.5, 23, 24] cm), ending with a WS row.

BO all sts.

Right Front

Work as for left front until piece measures about 10" (25.5 cm) from CO, ending with RS Row 3 of patt—23 (27, 29, 31, 35, 37) sts.

Shape Armhole

Keeping in patt, at armhole edge (beg of WS rows), BO 3 (4, 4, 4, 5, 5) sts at the beg of the next WS row, then BO 1 (2, 2, 2, 3, 3) st(s) at the beg of the foll 2 (1, 1, 2, 1, 1) WS row(s)—18 (21, 23, 23, 27, 29) sts rem.

BO 0 (1, 1, 1, 2, 2) st(s) at the beg of the next 0 (1, 2, 1, 1, 1) WS row(s), then BO 0 (0, 0, 0, 1, 1) st(s) at the beg of the foll 0 (0, 0, 0, 1, 2) WS row(s)—18 (20, 21, 22, 24, 25) sts rem.

Re-establish selvedge st at armhole edge and cont in patt until armhole measures 3 (3½, 4, 4½, 5, 5½)" (7.5 [9, 10, 11.5, 12.5, 14] cm), ending with a WS row.

Shape Neck

Keeping in patt, at neck edge (beg of RS rows), BO 4 sts once, then BO 2 (2, 3, 3, 3, 3) sts 2 (2, 1, 1, 1, 1) time(s), then BO 1 (1, 2, 2, 2, 2) st(s) 2 (2, 1, 1, 2, 2) time(s), then BO 0 (0, 1, 1, 1, 1) st 0 (0, 2, 2, 1, 1) time(s)—8 (10, 10, 11, 12, 13) sts rem.

Re-establish selvedge st at neck edge and cont in patt until armhole measures 7 (7½, 8, 8½, 9, 9½)" (18 [19, 20.5, 21.5, 23, 24] cm), ending with a WS row.

BO all sts.

Sleeves

With MC and using the I-cord method, CO 31 (35, 37, 41, 43, 45) sts. Cut yarn, leaving a 6" (15 cm) tail.

Slide CO sts to other needle tip so the first st CO will be the first st worked.

Next row: (RS) With MC, k1 (selvedge st; knit every row), k0 (0, 1, 1, 0, 1), pm, work Row 1 of bobble patt over center 29 (33, 33, 37, 41, 41) sts, pm, k0 (0, 1, 1, 0, 1), k1 (selvedge st; knit every row).

Keeping 1 edge st at each side in garter st and working any sts between selvedge sts and marked patt section in St st, work even in patt until piece measures about 10 (10, 10, 11¼, 11¼, 11¼)" (25.5 [25.5, 25.5, 28.5, 28.5, 28.5] cm) from CO, ending with WS Row 4 of patt.

Shape Cap

Keeping in patt, BO 3 (4, 4, 4, 5, 5) sts at the beg of the next 2 rows—25 (27, 29, 33, 33, 35) sts rem.

[BO 2 sts at the beg of the next 2 rows, then BO 1 st at the beg of the foll 2 rows] 2 (2, 1, 3, 3, 2) time(s)—13 (15, 23, 15, 15, 23) sts rem.

BO 1 st at the beg of the next 2 (4, 10, 2, 2, 8) rows, then BO 2 sts at the beg of the foll 2 rows—7 (7, 9, 9, 9, 11) sts rem.

BO all sts.

Finishing

Block to measurements (see Notes).

With yarn threaded on a tapestry needle, sew fronts to back at shoulders for 8 (10, 10, 11, 12, 13) sts, leaving center 21 (21, 23, 23, 25, 25) back neck sts unsewn. Sew side and sleeve seams with 1-st seam allowances (see Notes). Sew sleeve caps into armholes, matching center of cap BO with shoulder seam and matching sleeve seam with side seam at underarm.

Front and Neck Band

Notes: *An applied I-cord edging is worked from the lower right front corner, up the right front, around the neck opening, and down the left front to end at the lower left front corner. When you work the I-cord along the center front edges, join 5 I-cord rows for every 6 garment rows by *joining one I-cord row to 1 body row for 5 body rows, then skip the 6th body row; repeat from * to the end of the vertical edge. When you work I-cord along the shaped front neck edges, join the body rows and I-cord rows 1-for-1, without skipping any body rows. For the back neck, join each stitch to one I-cord row.*

With MC and dpn, CO 3 sts. With RS facing throughout and beg at lower right front corner, *slide sts to left needle tip, k2, sl last I-cord st purl-wise with yarn in back, yo, pick up and knit 1 st from garment edge, pass yo and sl st over picked-up st—3 I-cord sts rem; rep from * to end at lower left front corner. BO all sts.

Weave in loose ends.

Chapter 6

Accessories

Accessories are the final step in the ritual of dressing. Whether you're putting on a hat or choosing the right bag for your ensemble, accessories finish your look and make you stand out in a crowd. The three accessories in this chapter enhance your outfit and allow you to feel good when you step out of the house.

With the ability to transform an outfit from casual day to dreamy boho-chic, the *Cabrillo Felted Boho Hat* (page 146) looks good on all body types and with all face shapes. This hat achieves its sturdy, yet flouncy, shape from felting the finished knitted fabric. You'll be amazed at the ease and speed with which the Cabrillo will fly off your needles.

The functional style of the cross-body *Laren Felted Cross-Body Bag* (page 150) allows you to keep your day-to-day essentials with you on your daily travels. With its color-blocked felted fabric and the reinforced grommet openings that accommodate the metal strap, this bag is sturdy enough to carry everything you need. Although I worked mine in shades of purple and gray, the color combinations are endless. Let your imagination run wild when you knit this design.

The *Falkirk Plaid Wrap* (page 154) is an elegant way to add warmth to your outfit. The button detail along the top edge allows you to control the amount of drape you'd like around your neck. The plaid fabric is achieved by stranding the horizontal stripes and duplicate stitching the vertical stripes. Combined with the rustic feel of Shetland wool, Falkirk will become an easy favorite in your ritual of dressing.

Cabrillo

felted boho hat

Finished Size

About 21" (53.5 cm) head circumference, 42" (106.5 cm) brim circumference and 5" (12.5 cm) brim length, after felting.

Yarn

Worsted weight (#4 Medium).

Shown here: Stonehedge Fiber Mill Shepherd's Wool Yarn Worsted Weight (100% merino wool; 250 yd [229 m]/4 oz [113.5 g]): Plum, 2 skeins.

Needles

Size U.S. 10½ (6.5 mm): 24" (60 cm) circular (cir) and set of 4 double-pointed (dpn).

Adjust needle size if necessary to obtain the correct gauge.

Notions

Markers (m); tapestry needle; lingerie bag, old jeans (to help the felting process), and detergent for felting in washing machine.

Gauge

14 sts and 20 rnds = 4" (10 cm) in St st with two strands held together, before felting.

15 sts and 25 rnds = 4" (10 cm) in St st with two strands held together, after felting.

Knitted with two strands of worsted-weight yarn held together, this sturdy hat is worked in the round from the top of the crown to the wide brim. For the best results, shape the damp felted hat on a foam head or hat form and allow to air-dry thoroughly.

 Refer to Chapter 1 for general knitting foundations.

Hat

With dpn and holding two strands tog, CO 6 sts.

Arrange sts evenly on 3 dpn—2 sts per needle. Place marker (pm), and join for working in rnds, being careful not to twist sts.

Shape Crown

Rnd 1: Knit.

Rnd 2: [K1f&b (see Glossary), pm, k1f&b] 3 times—12 sts; 4 sts per needle.

Rnd 3: [K1f&b, knit to m, slip marker (sl m), k1f&b, knit to end of needle] 3 times—2 sts inc'd per needle.

Rnds 4–12: Rep Rnd 3 nine more times—72 sts; 24 sts per needle.

Rnds 13 and 14: Knit 2 rnds even.

Rnd 15: Rep Rnd 3 once more—78 sts; 26 sts per needle.

Knit every rnd until piece measures 8" (20.5 cm) from CO.

Shape Brim

Note: *Change to circular needle when there are too many stitches to fit comfortably on double-pointed needles.*

Rnd 1: (inc rnd) K1, [M1 (see Glossary), k4] 9 times, M1, k3, [M1, k4] 9 times, M1, k2—98 sts.

Rnds 2–8: Knit 7 rnds even.

Rnd 9: (inc rnd) K2, [M1, k5] 9 times, M1, k4, [M1, k5] 9 times, M1, k2—118 sts.

Rnds 10–16: Knit 7 rnds even.

Rnd 17: (inc rnd) K2, [M1, k6] 9 times, M1, k5, [M1, k6] 9 times, M1, k3—138 sts.

Rnds 18–24: Knit 7 rnds even.

Rnd 25: (inc rnd) K3, [M1, k7] 9 times, M1, k6, [M1, k7] 9 times, M1, k3—158 sts.

Rnds 26–32: Knit 7 rnds even—piece measures 14½" (37 cm) from CO.

BO all sts.

Finishing

Weave in loose ends.

Felting

Place hat in a lingerie bag and place bag in the washing machine, along with worn jeans or other laundry. Add a small amount of detergent and wash on the hottest setting. Felting time will depend on your machine and water conditions; monitor the progress every few minutes to prevent over-felting.

Remove hat from washer and handfelt specific areas as necessary to achieve an even surface.

Smooth hat over hat form and use pins to block brim into a flat circle. Allow to air-dry thoroughly before removing pins.

Laren

felted cross-body bag

Finished Size
About 11" (28 cm) wide, 7½" (19 cm) tall, and 2½" (6.5 cm) deep.

Yarn
Worsted weight (#4 Medium).

Shown here: Cascade 220 (100% wool; 220 yd [200 m]/100 g): #2410 Purple (MC), #8401 Silver Grey (CC1), and #9541 Lupin (CC2; light purple), 1 skein each.

Needles
Size U.S. 10½ (6.5 mm).

Adjust needle size if necessary to obtain the correct gauge.

Notions
Tapestry needle; two 1" (2.5 cm) grommets; grommet-setting tool, 1¼ yd (1.15 m) of ¾" (2 cm) chain, two ¾" (2 cm) sew-on snaps; two 1" (2.5 cm) metal D-rings.

Gauge
Note: All gauges are with two strands of the same color held together.

14 sts and 20 rows = 4" (10 cm) in St st, before felting.

15 sts and 24 rows = 4" (10 cm) in St st, after felting.

This bag is worked in five pieces, each with two strands of worsted-weight yarn held together in a color-block pattern. The pieces are felted to produce an extra-dense fabric that will withstand even heavy loads. A chain strap is secured through grommets and attached to D-rings to hold it in place. The flap closes with simple snaps.

notes

Work with two strands held together throughout.

Use a separate length of yarn for each color block and twist the yarns around each other at color changes to prevent holes from forming.

Refer to Chapter 1 for general knitting foundations.

Body

Holding two strands of CC1 tog, CO 42 sts. Work in St st (knit RS rows; purl WS rows) until piece measures 2" (5 cm) from CO, ending with a WS row.

Set-up row: (RS) Working with two strands of each color held tog throughout and twisting yarns at color changes (see Notes), k5 with CC1, k32 with MC, k5 with CC1.

Work each st in its established color until piece measures 19" (48.5 cm) from CO, ending with a WS row.

Change to CC1 and work even in St st until piece measures 21" (53.5 cm) from CO, ending with a WS row.

BO all sts.

Sides (Make 2)

Holding two strands of CC2 tog, CO 9 sts. Work in St st until piece measures 9" (23 cm) from CO, ending with a WS row.

BO all sts.

Top Flap

Holding two strands of CC1 tog, CO 42 sts. Work in St st until piece measures 2" (5 cm) from CO, ending with a WS row.

Set-up row: (RS) K5 with CC1, k32 with CC2, k5 with CC1.

Cont in St st color patt as established until piece measures 6½" (16.5 cm) from CO, ending with a WS row.

Next row: With CC1, k1, ssk, k3, change to CC2, k30, change to CC1, k3, k2tog, k1—40 sts rem.

Work even until piece measures 8¾" (22 cm) from CO, ending with a WS row.

Next row: With CC1, k1, ssk, knit to last 3 sts, k2tog, k1—38 sts rem.

Work even until piece measures 10½" (26.5 cm) from CO, ending with a WS row.

BO all sts.

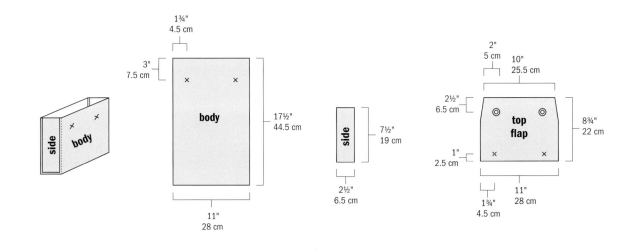

Shoulder Tab

Holding two strands of CC1 tog, CO 5 sts. Work in St st until piece measures 4" (10 cm) from CO.

BO all sts.

Finishing

Weave in loose ends.

Felting
Place pieces in a lingerie bag and place bag in the washing machine along with jeans or other laundry. Add a small amount of detergent and wash on the hottest setting.

Remove pieces and handfelt as necessary to achieve even surfaces.

Pin to measurements on a flat surface; shoulder strap not shown on schematic should measure about 1¼" (3.2 cm) wide and 3¼" (8.5 cm) high.

Allow to air-dry thoroughly before removing pins.

Grommets and Snaps
Mark placement for 2 grommets on top flap as indicated by circles on schematic. Affix grommets to bag according to manufacturer's instructions.

Sew female halves of snaps to RS of body front, centered on the Xs shown on schematic. Sew male halves of snaps to WS of top flap centered on Xs shown on schematic.

Assembly
With yarn threaded on a tapestry needle, sew each long edge of body along three edges of side piece as shown in diagram. Sew BO edge of top flap to upper back of body, with the flap inserted down into the body by about 1" (2.5 cm) so the back overlaps the flap.

Chain Strap
Cut chain into two equal pieces. Holding the two chain pieces together, insert one end down into a grommet in the top flap from RS to WS, then up through other grommet from WS to RS. Attach a D-ring to the doubled chain at each end to prevent the chain from slipping out of the grommets. Fold each short end of the shoulder tab around a D-ring by about ½" (1.3 cm) and sew securely in place with yarn threaded on a tapestry needle.

Falkirk
plaid wrap

Finished Size
About 64" (162.5 cm) wide and 14½" (37 cm) tall.

Yarn
Fingering weight (#1 Super Fine).

Shown here: Jamieson's Shetland Spindrift (100% Shetland wool; 115 yd [105 m]/25 g): #106 Mooskit (MC; tan), 6 balls; #726 Prussian Blue (CC1; dark blue); 5 balls, #135 Surf (CC2; light blue), 2 balls; #595 Maroon (CC3), 1 ball.

Needles
Size U.S. 3 (3.25 mm).

Adjust needle size if necessary to obtain the correct gauge.

Notions
Markers (m); tapestry needle; eleven ½" (1.3 cm) buttons.

Gauge
29 sts and 34 rnds = 4" (10 cm) in St st colorwork patt from Falkirk chart, worked in rnds.

This versatile rectangular wrap is worked in rounds with steek stitches that are cut open after the knitting is complete (see page 20)—the top edge is fastened with buttons; the steeks remain open at the side. The plaid design is worked in the stranded-colorwork technique, then additional single vertical red stitches are added with duplicate stitch.

Refer to Chapter 1 for general knitting foundations.

Wrap

With MC, CO 470 sts. Place marker (pm) and join for working in rnds, being careful not to twist sts.

Work even in St st (knit every rnd) until piece measures 1" (2.5 cm) from CO.

Next rnd: (hem fold line) Purl all sts through their back loops (tbl).

Work Rnds 1–27 of Falkirk chart 4 times, then work Rnds 1–12 once more.

Note: *The dotted lines shown on the chart are for reinforcing the steek later.*

Buttonhole rnd: (Rnd 13 of chart) Keeping in patt, *k19, work a [k2tog, yo] buttonhole; rep from * 10 more times, knit to end—11 buttonholes.

Work Rnds 14–16 of chart—124 chart rnds total; piece measures about 14½" (37 cm) from hem fold line.

Cut CCs and work to end of piece with MC only.

Next rnd: (hem fold line) *P1tbl; rep from *.

Work 3 rnds in St st.

Buttonhole rnd: *K19, work a [k2tog, yo] buttonhole; rep from * 10 more times, knit to end.

Cont in St st until piece measures 1" (2.5 cm) from fold line.

BO all sts.

Finishing

Duplicate-Stitch Embroidery
With CC3 threaded on a tapestry needle, work vertical lines of duplicate stitch (see page 20) as shown on chart.

Steek
Reinforce steek along the dotted lines shown on

chart (see page 20), then cut piece open in the center of the two reinforcement lines. Fold 4-st wide steeks to WS and sew in place as invisibly as possible with MC threaded on a tapestry needle.

Fold hems to WS along fold lines, taking care to match the buttonholes in both layers at the top. With MC threaded on a tapestry needle, sew hems in place, then work buttonhole st (see Glossary) to join the two layers of each buttonhole opening.

Block wrap into a rectangle 64" (162.5 cm) wide and 14½" (37 cm) tall.

Weave in loose ends.

Fold wrap in half, bringing short ends together with RS facing out, and lay it flat with the buttonhole edge running across the top—the buttonholes will all be in the same half. Using the buttonholes as a guide, mark the RS of the non-buttonhole half for 11 buttons aligned with the buttonholes, then sew buttons to marked positions.

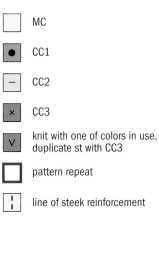

	MC
●	CC1
−	CC2
×	CC3
V	knit with one of colors in use, duplicate st with CC3
□	pattern repeat
!	line of steek reinforcement

FALKIRK

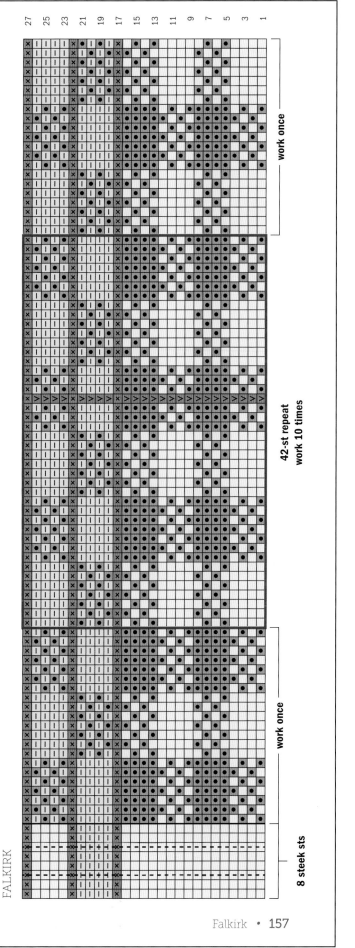

Glossary

Abbreviations

beg(s)	begin(s); beginning
BO	bind off
CC	contrast color
cir	circular
cm	centimeter(s)
cn	cable needle
CO	cast on
cont	continue(s); continuing
dec(s)('d)	decrease(s); decreasing; decreased
dpn	double-pointed needles
foll	follow(s); following
g	gram(s)
inc(s)('d)	increase(s); increasing; increase(d)
k	knit
k1f&b	knit into the front and back of the same stitch (increase)
k2tog	knit two stitches together (decrease)
kwise	knitwise, as if to knit
m	marker
mm	millimeter(s)
M1	make one stitch (increase)
M1P	make one stitch purlwise (increase)
oz	ounce
p	purl
p2tog	purl two stitches together (decrease)
patt(s)	pattern(s)
pm	place marker
psso	pass slipped stitch over
pwise	purlwise, as if to purl
rem	remain(s); remaining
rep	repeat(s); repeating
Rev St st	reverse stockinette stitch
rnd(s)	round(s)
RS	right side
sc	single crochet
sl	slip
ssk	slip, slip, knit (decrease)
st(s)	stitch(es)
St st	stockinette stitch
tbl	through back loop
tog	together
w&t	wrap and turn
WS	wrong side
wyb	with yarn in back
wyf	with yarn in front
yd	yard(s)
yo	yarnover
*	repeat starting point
* *	repeat all instructions between asterisks
( )	alternate measurements and/or instructions
[ ]	work instructions as a group a specified number of times

Bind-Offs

Standard Bind-Off

Knit the first stitch, *knit the next stitch (two stitches on right needle), insert left needle tip into first stitch on right needle (*Figure 1*) and lift this stitch up and over the second stitch (*Figure 2*) and off the needle (*Figure 3*). Repeat from * until one stitch remains on the right needle. Cut the yarn, leaving a 6" (15 cm) tail, then pull on the loop of the last stitch until the tail comes free to secure the last stitch.

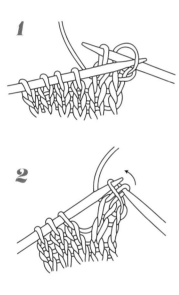

Buttonhole Stitch

Working into the edge half-stitch of the knitted piece, *bring tip of threaded needle in and out of a knitted stitch, place working yarn under needle tip, then bring threaded needle through the stitch and tighten. Repeat from *, always keeping the needle on top of the working yarn.

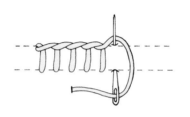

Cast-Ons

Backward-Loop Cast-On

*Loop working yarn and place it on needle backward so that it doesn't unwind. Repeat from *.

Crochet Provisional Cast-On

With waste yarn and crochet hook, make a loose crochet chain (see page 161) about four stitches more than you need to cast on. With knitting needle, working yarn, and beginning two stitches from end of chain, pick up and knit one stitch through the back loop of each crochet chain (*Figure 1*) for desired number of stitches. When you're ready to work in the opposite direction, pull out the crochet chain to expose live stitches (*Figure 2*).

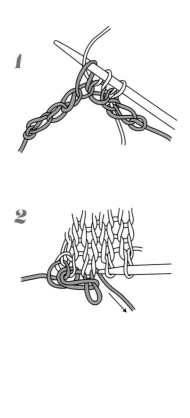

German Twisted (Old Norwegian) Cast-On

Leaving a long tail (about ½" [1.3 cm] for each stitch to be cast on), make a slipknot and place on the right needle. Place thumb and index finger of your left hand between the yarn ends so that working yarn is around your index finger and tail end is around your thumb and secure the yarn ends with your other fingers. Hold your palm upwards, making a V of yarn (*Figure 1*). *Bring needle in front of your thumb, under both yarns around your thumb, then down into the center of the thumb loop, forward in front of your thumb, and then over the top of the yarn around your index finger (*Figure 2*). Catching the yarn on your index finger, bring the needle back down through the thumb loop (*Figure 3*) and to the front, turning your thumb slightly to make space for the needle to pass through. Drop the loop off your thumb (*Figure 4*) and place your thumb back in the V configuration while tightening the resulting stitch on the needle (*Figure 5*). Repeat from * for the desired number of stitches.

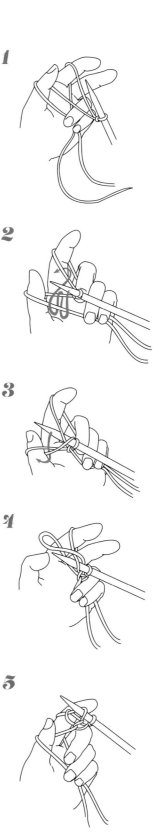

Long-Tail (Continental) Cast-On

Leaving a long tail (about ½" [1.3 cm] for each stitch to be cast on), make a slipknot and place on right needle. Place thumb and index finger of your left hand between the yarn ends so that working yarn is around your index finger and tail end is around your thumb and secure the yarn ends with your other fingers. Hold your palm upwards, making a V of yarn (*Figure 1*). *Bring needle up through loop on thumb (*Figure 2*), catch first strand around index finger, and go back down through loop on thumb (*Figure 3*). Drop loop off thumb and, placing thumb back in V configuration, tighten resulting stitch on needle (*Figure 4*). Repeat from * for the desired number of stitches.

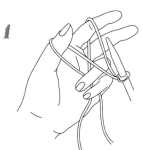

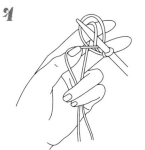

Crochet

Crochet Chain

Make a slipknot and place on crochet hook. *Yarn over hook and draw through a loop on the hook. Repeat from * for the desired number of stitches. To fasten off, cut yarn and draw end through last loop made.

Single Crochet (sc)

*Insert hook into the second chain from the hook (or the next stitch), yarn over hook and draw through a loop, yarn over hook (*Figure 1*), and draw it through both loops on hook (*Figure 2*). Repeat from * for the desired number of stitches.

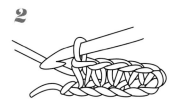

Decreases

Knit 2 Together (k2tog)

Knit two stitches together as if they were a single stitch.

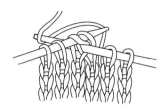

Purl 2 Together (p2tog)

Purl two stitches together as if they were a single stitch.

Slip, Slip, Knit (ssk)

Slip two stitches individually knitwise (*Figure 1*), insert left needle tip into the front of these two slipped stitches, and use the right needle to knit them together through their back loops (*Figure 2*).

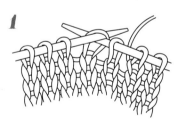

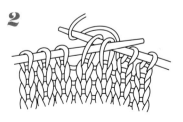

Increases

Bar Increases

Knitwise (k1f&b)

Knit into a stitch but leave the stitch on the left needle (*Figure 1*), then knit through the back loop of the same stitch (*Figure 2*) and slip the original stitch off the needle (*Figure 3*).

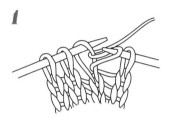

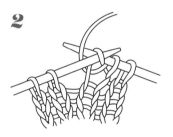

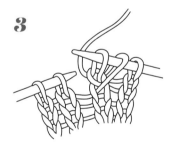

Purlwise (p1f&b)

Work as for a knitwise bar increase, but purl into the front and back of the same stitch.

Raised Make-One Increases

Knitwise (M1)

With left needle tip, lift the strand between the last knitted stitch and the first stitch on the left needle from front to back (*Figure 1*), then knit the lifted loop through the back (*Figure 2*).

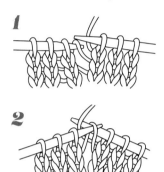

Purlwise (M1P)

Work as for knitwise make-one increase, but purl the lifted loop.

Pick Up and Purl

With wrong side of work facing and working from right to left, *insert the needle tip under both legs of the selvedge stitch from the far side to the near side (*Figure 1*), wrap yarn around needle, then pull a loop through to the back (*Figure 2*). Repeat from * for the specified number of stitches.

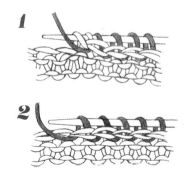

Seams

Backstitch Seam

Pin pieces to be seamed with right sides facing together. Working from right to left into the edge stitches, bring threaded needle up between the next two stitches on each piece of knitted fabric, then back down through both layers, one stitch to the right of the starting point (*Figure 1*). *Bring the needle up through both layers one stitch to the left of the backstitch just made (*Figure 2*), then back down to the right, through the same hole used before (*Figure 3*). Repeat from *, working backward one stitch for every two stitches worked forward.

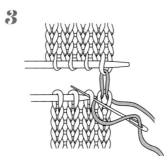

Kitchener-Stitch Grafting

Arrange stitches on two needles so that there is the same number of stitches on each needle. Hold the needles parallel to each other with wrong sides of the knitting facing together. Allowing about ½" (1.3 cm) per stitch to be grafted, thread matching yarn on a tapestry needle. Work from right to left as follows:

Step 1. Bring tapestry needle through the first stitch on the front needle as if to purl and leave the stitch on the needle (*Figure 1*).

Step 2. Bring tapestry needle through the first stitch on the back needle as if to knit and leave that stitch on the needle (*Figure 2*).

Step 3. Bring tapestry needle through the first front stitch as if to knit and slip this stitch off the needle, then bring the tapestry needle through the next front stitch as if to purl and leave this stitch on the needle (*Figure 3*).

Step 4. Bring tapestry needle through the first back stitch as if to purl and slip this stitch off the needle, then bring the tapestry needle through the next back stitch as if to knit and leave this stitch on the needle (*Figure 4*).

Repeat Steps 3 and 4 until one stitch remains on each needle, adjusting the tension to match the rest of the knitting as you go. To finish, bring the tapestry needle through the front stitch as if to knit and slip this stitch off the needle, then bring the tapestry needle through the back stitch as if to purl and slip this stitch off the needle.

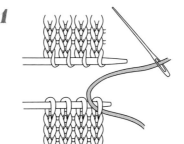

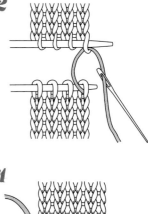

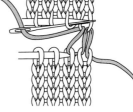

Running-Stitch Seam

Bring threaded needle in and out through both layers, forming a dashed line.

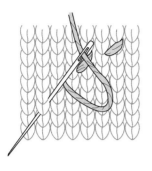

Whipstitch Seam

Hold pieces to be sewn together so that the edges to be seamed are aligned with each other. With yarn threaded on a tapestry needle, *insert needle through both layers from back to front, then bring needle to back. Repeat from *, keeping even tension on the seaming yarn.

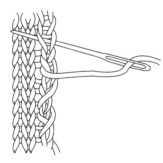

Short-Rows

Short-Rows Knit Side

Work to turning point, slip next stitch purlwise (*Figure 1*), bring the yarn to the front, then slip the same stitch back to the left needle (*Figure 2*), turn the work around and bring the yarn in position for the next stitch—one stitch has been wrapped, and the yarn is correctly positioned to work the next stitch.

When you come to a wrapped stitch on a subsequent row, hide the wrap by working it together with the wrapped stitch as follows: insert right needle tip under the wrap (from the front if wrapped stitch is a knit stitch; from the back if wrapped stitch is a purl stitch; *Figure 3*), then into the stitch on the needle, and work the stitch and its wrap together as a single stitch.

1

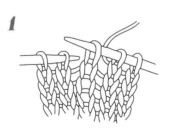

2

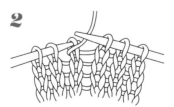

3

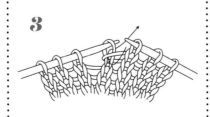

Short-Rows Purl Side

Work to the turning point, slip the next stitch purlwise to the right needle, bring the yarn to the back of the work (*Figure 1*), return the slipped stitch to the left needle, bring the yarn to the front between the needles (*Figure 2*), and turn the work so that the knit side is facing—one stitch has been wrapped, and the yarn is correctly positioned to knit the next stitch.

To hide the wrap on a subsequent purl row, work to the wrapped stitch, use the tip of the right needle to pick up the wrap from the back, place it on the left needle (*Figure 3*), then purl it together with the wrapped stitch.

1

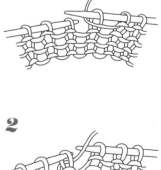

2

3

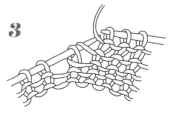

Buttons, Notions, and Zippers

Blumenthal Lansing Co.
buttonlovers.com
- large selection of buttons

Botani Trimmings
botanitrim.com
- custom zippers

Jo-Ann Fabric
joann.com
- wide assortment of fabrics and notions

M&J Trimming
mjtrim.com
- large selection of buttons, zippers, chains, and other notions

Pacific Trimming
pacifictrimming.com
- large selection of buttons, zippers, chains, and other notions

Knitting Tips and Video Tutorials

Interweave Knits
interweaveknits.com
- helpful knitting tips and other knitting resources

Worldknits
worldknits.com
- knitting calculators, video tutorials, and helpful knitting tips from the author, Alex Capshaw-Taylor

Yarns

ArtYarns
70 Westmoreland Ave.
White Plains, NY 10606
artyarns.com

Berroco Inc.
1 Tupperware Dr. Ste. 4
North Smithfield, RI 02896
berroco.com

Cascade Yarns
PO Box 58168
1224 Andover Park E.
Tukwila, WA 98188
cascadeyarns.com

Knitting Fever Inc./Louisa Harding/Katia
PO Box 336
315 Bayview Ave.
Amityville, NY 11701
knittingfever.com

Malabrigo
malabrigoyarn.com

Madelinetosh
3430 Alemeda St., Ste. 112
Fort Worth, TX 76126
madelinetosh.com

Simply Shetland/Jamieson's of Shetland
18375 Olympic Ave. S.
Seattle, WA 98188
simplyshetland.net

Stonehedge Fiber Mill
2246 Pesek Rd.
East Jordan, MI 49727
stonehedgefibermill.com

Westminster Fibers/Rowan
165 Ledge St.
Nashua, NH 03060
westminsterfibers.com

Bibliography

Knight, Erika, ed. *Cables & Arans: 250 Stitches to Knit*. Loveland, Colorado: Interweave, 2007. Harmony Guides.

_____., *Knit & Purl: 250 Stitches to Knit*. Loveland, Colorado: Interweave, 2007. Harmony Guides.

_____., *Lace & Eyelets: 250 Stitches to Knit*. Loveland, Colorado: Interweave, 2007. Harmony Guides.

Paden, Shirley. *Knitwear Design Workshop: A Comprehensive Guide to Handknits*. Loveland, Colorado: Interweave, 2009.

Sease, Cap. *Cast On, Bind Off: 211 Ways to Begin and End Your Knitting*. Bothell, Washington: Martingale, 2012.

Walker, Barbara G. *A Treasury of Knitting Patterns*. Pittsville, Wisconsin: Schoolhouse Press, 1998.

_____., *A Second Treasury of Knitting Patterns*. Pittsville, Wisconsin: Schoolhouse Press, 1998.

Index

So much to knit, so little time!

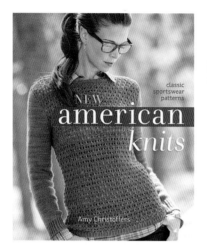

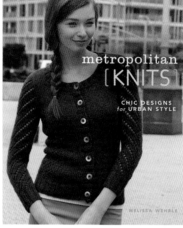

New American Knits
Classic Sportswear Patterns
Amy Christoffers
ISBN 978-1-62033-099-9
$24.99

Metropolitan Knits
Chic Designs for Urban Styles
Melissa Wehrle
ISBN 978-1-59668-778-3
$24.95

Wanderlust
46 Modern Knits for Bohemian Style
Tanis Gray
ISBN 978-1-62033-8315
$18.99

Interweave Knits magazine inspires and informs the modern knitter with projects and articles that celebrate the handmade life. Each issue features lush projects from your favorite designers, in-depth technique articles to further your knitting knowledge, information on the latest must-have yarns, designer profiles, and much more.
interweaveknits.com

Knitting Daily is a community for knitters who want inspiration, innovation, motivation, knitting content, and patterns for all levels and interests.
knittingdaily.com